THIRD EDITION

3

Skills for Success

LISTENING AND SPEAKING

Miles Craven | Kristin Donnalley Sherman

OXFORD

UNIVERSITY PRESS

OXFORD
UNIVERSITY PRESS

198 Madison Avenue
New York, NY 10016 USA

Great Clarendon Street, Oxford, OX2 6DP, United Kingdom

Oxford University Press is a department of the University of Oxford.
It furthers the University's objective of excellence in research, scholarship,
and education by publishing worldwide. Oxford is a registered trade
mark of Oxford University Press in the UK and in certain other countries

ISBN: 978 0 19 490515 2 (STUDENT BOOK 3 WITH IQ ONLINE PACK)
ISBN: 978 0 19 490503 9 (STUDENT BOOK 3 AS PACK COMPONENT)
ISBN: 978 0 19 490539 8 (Q ONLINE STUDENT WEBSITE)

Printed in China

This book is printed on paper from certified and well-managed sources

ACKNOWLEDGEMENTS

Back cover photograph: Oxford University Press building/David Fisher

*The author and publisher are grateful to those who have given permission to
reproduce the following extracts and adaptations of copyright material:*
p. 158 from "Happiness Breeds Success ... and Money!" by Sonja
Lyubomirsky, 18 July 2008, www.psychologytoday.com. Reproduced by
permission.

Illustration by: p. 83 Phil Hackett/Eyecandy

*We would also like to thank the following for permission to reproduce the following
photographs:* **123RF:** p. 42 (two runners stretching/langstrup); **Alamy:**
pp. 8 (woman with cold/Rob Lewine), 28 (spice stall/Ilya Paripsa), 39 (sea
view restaurant/Helmut Corneli), 51 (women eating fries/Geoff Smith),
76 (advertising in city/Ken Howard), 87 (airport trolleys/imageBROKER),
90 (advertising posters/B.O'Kane), 93 (adverts in a grocery circular/B
Christopher), 112 (volcanologist/tom pfeiffer), 118 (hikers in rain/
Catalin Petolea), 133 (man playing chess against robot/ZUMA Press,
Inc.), 150 (yacht outside expensive house/LOOK Die Bildagentur der
Fotografen GmbH), 182 (deep sea submersible/Jeff Rotman), 186 (flooded
neighborhood/PJF Military Collection); **Getty:** pp. cover (small island
with buildings at Ezhikara,Kerala India/gulfu photography), 2 (woman
putting on make up/Trevor Williams), 5 (smiling barista/J James/Corbis),
7 (woman shaking hands/Daniel Tardif), 11 (student reading book/Seb
Oliver), 13 (Malcolm Gladwell/Bloomberg), 13 (Daniel Kahneman/Andreas
Rentz), 15 (friends socialising on steps/Caiaimage/Sam Edwards), 17
(young adult shaking hands/Delmaine Donson), 18 (tourist and stallholder/
Andrew Watson), 25 (men dressed in colourful suits/Grant Faint), 26
(family preparing food in kitchen/DGLimages), 35 (man eating apple/
franckreporter), 38 (Icelandic food/Cultura), 44 (women drinking coffee/
AntonioGuillem), 52 (couple in mobile home/Tony Anderson),

55 (Jeffrey Skoll/Mike Windle), 57 (eBay HQ/Justin Sullivan), 60 (Barbara
Ehrenreich/Bloomberg), 63 (female supermarket clerk/Jeffrey Greenberg),
75 (girl and father loading car /kali9), 78 (children watching television/
Hero Images), 79 (Sesame Street merchandise/EDUARDO MUNOZ
ALVAREZ), 88 (advertising on screen/VIEW press), 89 (advertising in
lights/Maremagnum), 99 (Times Square advertising/Brigitte Blättler), 100
(man filming lava flow/Arctic-Images), 102 (two people canoeing/Kerrick
James), 106 (teenagers in car/franckreporter), 110 (filming tornado/
Carsten Peter), 114 (artwork of Megellan's ship/Bjorn Landstrom), 120
(young male in Japan/Imagesource), 125 (ship on roughs seas/Christopher
Pillitz), 128 (self-driving car/JasonDoiy), 131 (two dolphins/J & C Sohns),
134 (rover, Curiosity/Anadolu Agency), 138 (Colossus computer/Bletchley
Park Trust), 140 (girl looking at rain/PeopleImages), 144 (students
discussing work/Peter Muller), 149 (engineer with robot/Matt Cardy),
152 (expensive car/Mlenny), 154 (view of Truro in Nova Scotia/Barrett &
MacKay), 155 (antique vase/Fotosearch), 157 (woman flower arranging/
Robert Alexander), 158 (woman in workshop/Maskot), 160 (group of work
colleagues laughing/Luis Alvarez), 172 (camping by lake/Thomas Barwick),
176 (students reading exam results/Hero Images), 177 (J.K. Rowling/
Samir Hussein), 179 (Edison lightbulb/HighImpactPhotography), 189
(woman firing arrow/myshkovsky), 192 (professor presenting to students/
David Schaffer), 197 (soccer team celebrating win/simonkr); **OUP:** pp.
35 (boy disgusted at food/Shutterstock), 40 (Japanese food/Shutterstock),
173 (expensive house/123RF); **Reuters:** pp. 126 (robot/Benoir Tessier);
Shutterstock: pp. 10 (college students/YAKOBCHUK VIACHESLAV), 19
(woman buying coat/frantic00), 22 (two students shaking hands/Helder
Almeida), 30 (salt/CKP1001), 30 (wattle seed/KarenHBlack), 30 (turmeric/
spicyPXL), 36 (Mediterranean food/gorillaimages), 41 (fresh lemonade/
Carol Mellema), 43 (sliced chilli/flashgun), 46 (chopped vegetables/Africa
Studio), 47 (rice porridge/Alexander Prokopenko), 47 (bluberries on
bush/Trong Nguyen), 48 (spaghetti with red sauce/DronG), 50 (salad bar/
kitzcorner), 59 (Frank Lloyd Wright home/Sean Pavone), 65 (clothes design
studio/Rawpixel.com), 69 (Paris skyline/lassedesignen), 70 (scuba diver/
Jukkis), 72 (people whitewater rafting/Strahil Dimitrov), 81 (Pokemon
merchandise/canyalcin), 104 (snowboarder/Dmytro Vietrov), 105 (baby
taing first steps/Monkey Business Images), 122 (man photographing the
colloseum/WineDonuts), 129 (astronaut on the moon/Shutterstock), 134
(robot, Sophia/Shutterstock), 138 (Alan Turing/Shutterstock); 142 (smart
speaker/Mayuree Moonhirun), 153 (stack of dollar notes/Solcan Design),
165 (view of Sydney harbor/Kelvin Shutter), 168 (couple in argument/
Iakov Filimonov), 170 (Chaing Mai/Take Photo), 174 (woman outside her
business/Rawpixel.com), 177 (Ang Lee/Featureflash Photo Agency), 177
(Thomas Edison/Everett Historical), 180 (removing burnt food from oven/
Fotos593), 185 (paralympic skier/MikeDotta); **Third party:** pp. 159 (Sonja
Lyubomirsky/Josh Blanchard), 182 (Mohannad Abu-dayyah/Mohannad
Abu-Dayyah)

ACKNOWLEDGMENTS

We would like to acknowledge the teachers from all over the world who participated in the development process and review of *Q: Skills for Success* Third Edition.

USA

Kate Austin, Avila University, MO; **Sydney Bassett**, Auburn Global University, AL; **Michael Beamer**, USC, CA; **Renae Betten**, CBU, CA; **Pepper Boyer**, Auburn Global University, AL; **Marina Broeder**, Mission College, CA; **Thomas Brynmore**, Auburn Global University, AL; **Britta Burton**, Mission College, CA; **Kathleen Castello**, Mission College, CA; **Teresa Cheung**, North Shore Community College, MA; **Shantall Colebrooke**, Auburn Global University, AL; **Kyle Cooper**, Troy University, AL; **Elizabeth Cox**, Auburn Global University, AL; **Ashley Ekers**, Auburn Global University, AL; **Rhonda Farley**, Los Rios Community College, CA; **Marcus Frame**, Troy University, AL; **Lora Glaser**, Mission College, CA; **Hala Hamka**, Henry Ford College, MI; **Shelley A. Harrington**, Henry Ford College, MI; **Barrett J. Heusch**, Troy University, AL; **Beth Hill**, St. Charles Community College, MO; **Patty Jones**, Troy University, AL; **Tom Justice**, North Shore Community College, MA; **Robert Klein**, Troy University, AL; **Patrick Maestas**, Auburn Global University, AL; **Elizabeth Merchant**, Auburn Global University, AL; **Rosemary Miketa**, Henry Ford College, MI; **Myo Myint**, Mission College, CA; **Lance Noe**, Troy University, AL; **Irene Pannatier**, Auburn Global University, AL; **Annie Percy**, Troy University, AL; **Erin Robinson**, Troy University, AL; **Juliane Rosner**, Mission College, CA; **Mary Stevens**, North Shore Community College, MA; **Pamela Stewart**, Henry Ford College, MI; **Karen Tucker**, Georgia Tech, GA; **Loreley Wheeler**, North Shore Community College, MA; **Amanda Wilcox**, Auburn Global University, AL; **Heike Williams**, Auburn Global University, AL

Canada

Angelika Brunel, Collège Ahuntsic, QC; **David Butler**, English Language Institute, BC; **Paul Edwards**, Kwantlen Polytechnic University, BC; **Cody Hawver**, University of British Columbia, BC; **Olivera Jovovic**, Kwantlen Polytechnic University, BC; **Tami Moffatt**, University of British Columbia, BC; **Dana Pynn**, Vancouver Island University, BC

Latin America

Georgette Barreda, SENATI, Peru; **Claudia Cecilia Díaz Romero**, Colegio América, Mexico; **Jeferson Ferro**, Uninter, Brazil; **Mayda Hernández**, English Center, Mexico; **Jose Ixtaccihusatl**, Instituto Tecnológico de Tecomatlán, Mexico; **Andreas Paulus Pabst**, CBA Idiomas, Brazil; **Amanda Carla Pas**, Instituição de Ensino Santa Izildinha, Brazil; **Allen Quesada Pacheco**, University of Costa Rica, Costa Rica; **Rolando Sánchez**, Escuela Normal de Tecámac, Mexico; **Luis Vasquez**, CESNO, Mexico

Asia

Asami Atsuko, Jissen Women's University, Japan; **Rene Bouchard**, Chinzei Keiai Gakuen, Japan; **Francis Brannen**, Sangmyung University, South Korea; **Haeyun Cho**, Sogang University, South Korea; **Daniel Craig**, Sangmyung University, South Korea; **Thomas Cuming**, Royal Melbourne Institute of Technology, Vietnam; **Nguyen Duc Dat**, OISP, Vietnam; **Wayne Devitte**, Tokai University, Japan; **James D. Dunn**, Tokai University, Japan; **Fergus Hann**, Tokai University, Japan; **Michael Hood**, Nihon University College of Commerce, Japan; **Hideyuki Kashimoto**, Shijonawate High School, Japan; **David Kennedy**, Nihon University, Japan; **Anna Youngna Kim**, Sogang University, South Korea; **Jae Phil Kim**, Sogang University, South Korea; **Jaganathan Krishnasamy**, GB Academy, Malaysia; **Peter Laver**, Incheon National University, South Korea; **Hung Hoang Le**, Ho Chi Minh City University of Technology, Vietnam; **Hyon Sook Lee**, Sogang University, South Korea; **Ji-seon Lee**, Iruda English Institute, South Korea; **Joo Young Lee**, Sogang University, South Korea; **Phung Tu Luc**, Ho Chi Minh City University of Technology, Vietnam; **Richard Mansbridge**, Hoa Sen University, Vietnam; **Kahoko Matsumoto**, Tokai University, Japan; **Elizabeth May**, Sangmyung University, South Korea; **Naoyuki Naganuma**, Tokai University, Japan; **Hiroko Nishikage**, Taisho University, Japan; **Yongjun Park**, Sangji University, South Korea; **Paul Rogers**, Dongguk University, South Korea; **Scott Schafer**, Inha University, South Korea; **Michael Schvaudner**, Tokai University, Japan; **Brendan Smith**, RMIT University, School of Languages and English, Vietnam; **Peter Snashall**, Huachiew Chalermprakiet University, Thailand; **Makoto Takeda**, Sendai Third Senior High School, Japan; **Peter Talley**, Mahidol University, Faculty of ICT, Thailand; **Byron Thigpen**, Sogang University, South Korea; **Junko Yamaai**, Tokai University, Japan; **Junji Yamada**, Taisho University, Japan; **Sayoko Yamashita**, Jissen Women's University, Japan; **Masami Yukimori**, Taisho University, Japan

Middle East and North Africa

Sajjad Ahmad, Taibah University, Saudi Arabia; **Basma Alansari**, Taibah University, Saudi Arabia; **Marwa Al-ashqar**, Taibah University, Saudi Arabia; **Dr. Rashid Al-Khawaldeh**, Taibah University, Saudi Arabia; **Mohamed Almohamed**, Taibah University, Saudi Arabia; **Dr Musaad Alrahaili**, Taibah University, Saudi Arabia; **Hala Al Sammar**, Kuwait University, Kuwait; **Ahmed Alshammari**, Taibah University, Saudi Arabia; **Ahmed Alshamy**, Taibah University, Saudi Arabia; **Doniazad sultan AlShraideh**, Taibah University, Saudi Arabia; **Sahar Amer**, Taibah University, Saudi Arabia; **Nabeela Azam**, Taibah University, Saudi Arabia; **Hassan Bashir**, Edex, Saudi Arabia; **Rachel Batchilder**, College of the North Atlantic, Qatar; **Nicole Cuddie**, Community College of Qatar, Qatar; **Mahdi Duris**, King Saud University, Saudi Arabia; **Ahmed Ege**, Institute of Public Administration, Saudi Arabia; **Magda Fadle**, Victoria College, Egypt; **Mohammed Hassan**, Taibah University, Saudi Arabia; **Tom Hodgson**, Community College of Qatar, Qatar; **Ayub Agbar Khan**, Taibah University, Saudi Arabia; **Cynthia Le Joncour**, Taibah University, Saudi Arabia; **Ruari Alexander MacLeod**, Community College of Qatar, Qatar; **Nasir Mahmood**, Taibah University, Saudi Arabia; **Duria Salih Mahmoud**, Taibah University, Saudi Arabia; **Ameera McKoy**, Taibah University, Saudi Arabia; **Chaker Mhamdi**, Buraimi University College, Oman; **Baraa Shiekh Mohamed**, Community College of Qatar, Qatar; **Abduleelah Mohammed**, Taibah University, Saudi Arabia; **Shumaila Nasir**, Taibah University, Saudi Arabia; **Kevin Onwordi**, Taibah University, Saudi Arabia; **Dr. Navid Rahmani**, Community College of Qatar, Qatar; **Dr. Sabah Salman Sabbah**, Community College of Qatar, Qatar; **Salih**, Taibah University, Saudi Arabia; **Verna Santos-Nafrada**, King Saud University, Saudi Arabia; **Gamal Abdelfattah Shehata**, Taibah University, Saudi Arabia; **Ron Stefan**, Institute of Public Administration, Saudi Arabia; **Dr. Saad Torki**, Imam Abdulrahman Bin Faisal University, Dammam, Saudi Arabia; **Silvia Yafai**, Applied Technology High School/Secondary Technical School, UAE; **Mahmood Zar**, Taibah University, Saudi Arabia; **Thouraya Zheni**, Taibah University, Saudi Arabia

Turkey

Sema Babacan, Istanbul Medipol University; **Bilge Çöllüoğlu Yakar**, Bilkent University; **Liana Corniel**, Koc University; **Savas Geylanioglu**, Izmir Bahcesehir Science and Technology College; **Öznur Güler**, Giresun University; **Selen Bilginer Halefoğlu**, Maltepe University; **Ahmet Konukoğlu**, Hasan Kalyoncu University; **Mehmet Salih Yoğun**, Gaziantep Hasan Kalyoncu University; **Fatih Yücel**, Beykent University

Europe

Amina Al Hashamia, University of Exeter, UK; **Irina Gerasimova**, Saint-Petersburg Mining University, Russia; **Jodi**, Las Dominicas, Spain; **Marina Khanykova**, School 179, Russia; **Oksana Postnikova**, Lingua Practica, Russia; **Nina Vasilchenko**, Soho-Bridge Language School, Russia

CRITICAL THINKING

The unique critical thinking approach of the *Q: Skills for Success* series has been further enhanced in the Third Edition. New features help you analyze, synthesize, and develop your ideas.

Unit question
The thought-provoking unit questions engage you with the topic and provide a critical thinking framework for the unit.

? UNIT QUESTION

Can money buy happiness?

A. Discuss these questions with your classmates.

1. How much money do you think people really need in order to be happy? Explain.
2. Do you think more money would make you happier? Why or why not?
3. Look at the photo. Would you be happier if you could buy a home like this? Why or why not?

Analysis
You can discuss your opinion of each listening text and analyze how it changes your perspective on the unit question.

? SAY WHAT YOU THINK

SYNTHESIZE Think about Listening 1, Listening 2, and the unit video as you discuss the questions.

1. What is the difference between sudden wealth and earning more money from a better job? Which would you prefer? Why?
2. Who do you think is more responsible for poverty—the wealthy or the poor themselves? Why do you think so?
3. How does wealth, whether you earn it, get it from family, or receive it suddenly, separate people?

NEW! Critical Thinking Strategy with video
Each unit includes a Critical Thinking Strategy with activities to give you step-by-step guidance in critical analysis of texts. An accompanying instructional video (available on iQ Online) provides extra support and examples.

CRITICAL THINKING STRATEGY

Summarizing information you hear

When you **summarize** information that you hear, you give the main points but not all the details. You have to decide what information is important and what is not. Also, you find shorter ways to express information. This means that summaries are in your own words, not copied from the source.

College professors commonly require summaries—on tests or as part of homework assignments—as indications that you understood a listening passage. You can practice writing summaries on your own. After you have finished listening to any passage that is a minute or two long, write a summary of it for yourself. Then show your summary to a friend. Ask if your friend can understand what you heard just by reading or listening to the summary. If not, ask what other information your friend would want to know.

iQ PRACTICE Go online to watch the Critical Thinking Video and check your comprehension. *Practice > Unit 3 > Activity 7*

D. SYNTHESIZE Work with a partner. Listen again and take notes on what the speakers say about each book. Then write a summary of about 75 words about Barbara Ehrenreich's work. Your summary should mention both books.

E. DISCUSS Discuss the questions in a group.

1. Why do you think *Nickel and Dimed* was a best seller?
2. What qualities do you think a person needs to go undercover as Ehrenreich did? Would you like to try doing this? Why or why not?

NEW! Bloom's Taxonomy
Blue activity headings integrate verbs from Bloom's Taxonomy to help you see how each activity develops critical thinking skills.

THREE TYPES OF VIDEO

UNIT VIDEO

The unit videos include high-interest documentaries and reports on a wide variety of subjects, all linked to the unit topic and question.

NEW! "Work with the Video" pages guide you in watching, understanding, and discussing the unit videos. The activities help you see the connection to the Unit Question and the other texts in the unit.

NEW! In some units, one of the main listening texts is a video.

CRITICAL THINKING VIDEO

NEW! Narrated by the *Q* series authors, these short videos give you further instruction on the Critical Thinking Strategy of each unit using engaging images and graphics. You can use them to gain a deeper understanding of the Critical Thinking Strategy.

SKILLS VIDEO

NEW! These instructional videos provide illustrated explanations of skills and grammar points in the Student Book. They can be viewed in class or assigned for a flipped classroom, for homework, or for review. One skill video is available for every unit.

Easily access all videos in the Resources section of iQ Online.

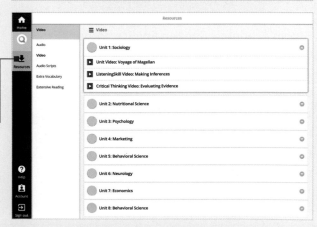

VOCABULARY

A research-based vocabulary program focuses on the words you need to know academically and professionally.

The vocabulary syllabus in *Q: Skills for Success* is correlated to the CEFR (see page 198) and linked to two word lists: the Oxford 3000 and the OPAL (Oxford Phrasal Academic Lexicon).

⚷ OXFORD 3000

The Oxford 3000 lists the core words that every learner at the A1–B2 level needs to know. Items in the word list are selected for their frequency and usefulness from the Oxford English Corpus (a database of over 2 billion words).

Vocabulary Key
In vocabulary activities, ⚷ shows you the word is in the Oxford 3000 and **OPAL** shows you the word or phrase is in the OPAL.

PREVIEW THE LISTENING

A. PREVIEW The interviewer's first question is, "So, are machines now as smart as we are?" What do you think? Discuss your ideas with a partner. Take notes on your discussion.

B. VOCABULARY Read aloud these words from Listening 1. Check (✓) the ones you know. Use a dictionary to define any new or unknown words. Then discuss with a partner how the words will relate to the unit.

automated *(adj.)*	layer *(n.)* ⚷	reject *(v.)* ⚷ OPAL
clever *(adj.)* ⚷	obvious *(adj.)* ⚷ OPAL	stand by *(v. phr.)*
fair *(adj.)* ⚷	predictable *(adj.)*	take over *(v. phr.)*
figure out *(v. phr.)*		

⚷ Oxford 3000™ words   OPAL Oxford Phrasal Academic Lexicon

iQ PRACTICE Go online to listen and practice your pronunciation.
Practice > Unit 6 > Activity 2

OPAL
OXFORD PHRASAL ACADEMIC LEXICON

NEW! The OPAL is a collection of four word lists that provide an essential guide to the most important words and phrases to know for academic English. The word lists are based on the Oxford Corpus of Academic English and the British Academic Spoken English corpus. The OPAL includes both spoken and written academic English and both individual words and longer phrases.

Academic Language tips in the Student Book give information about how words and phrases from the OPAL are used and offer help with features such as collocations and phrases.

ACADEMIC LANGUAGE
The corpus shows that speakers use *is important to . . .* to draw attention to something. The lecturer in Listening 2 uses this phrase to draw attention to why Alan Turing created the Turing Test.

―――――― **OPAL**
Oxford Phrasal Academic Lexicon

1. In an earlier class, the students had learned not to were smarter because the answer is always: _____
   a. it depends on what one means by "smart"
   b. AI cannot possibly match humans
   c. humans can't manage as much information as

2. The students and professor make a few mistakes _
   a. in remembering whether Sophia is a woman or
   b. in deciding whether Sophia is good or bad
   c. in using the correct pronoun to refer to Sophia

3. One thing Sophia is famous for is _____ .
   a. being smarter than any other AI device
   b. having a real human body
   c. being named a citizen of a real country

4. One purpose of social robots is to _____ .
   a. spend time with and talk to people in places lik
   b. learn to play games like chess better than huma
   c. solve difficult problems between countries and

EXTENSIVE READING

NEW! Extensive Reading is a program of reading for pleasure at a level that matches your language ability.

There are many benefits to Extensive Reading:

- It helps you to become a better reader in general.
- It helps to increase your reading speed.
- It can improve your reading comprehension.
- It increases your vocabulary range.
- It can help you improve your grammar and writing skills.
- It's great for motivation to read something that is interesting for its own sake.

Each unit of *Q: Skills for Success* Third Edition has been aligned to an Oxford Graded Reader based on the appropriate topic and level of language proficiency. The first chapter of each recommended graded reader can be downloaded from iQ Online Resources.

What is iQ ONLINE?

iQ ONLINE extends your learning beyond the classroom.

- Practice activities provide essential skills practice and support.
- Automatic grading and progress reports show you what you have mastered and where you need more practice.
- The Discussion Board allows you to discuss the Unit Questions and helps you develop your critical thinking.
- Essential resources such as audio and video are easy to access anytime.

NEW TO THE THIRD EDITION

- iQ Online is optimized for mobile use so you can use it on your phone.
- An updated interface allows easy navigation around the activities, tests, resources, and scores.
- New Critical Thinking Videos expand on the Critical Thinking Strategies in the Student Book.
- The Extensive Reading program helps you improve your vocabulary and reading skills.

How to use iQ ONLINE

Go to **Practice** to find additional practice and support to complement your learning in the classroom.

Go to **Resources** to find:
- All Student Book video
- All Student Book audio
- Critical Thinking videos
- Skills videos
- Extensive Reading

Go to **Messages** and **Discussion Board** to communicate with your teacher and classmates.

Online tests assigned by your teacher help you assess your progress and see where you need more practice.

A progress bar shows you how many activities you have completed.

View your scores for all activities.

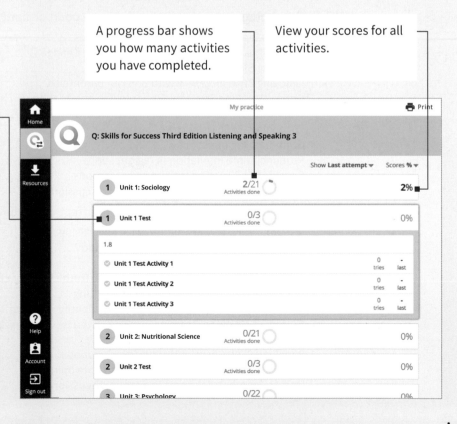

CONTENTS

Sociology

Are first impressions accurate?

A. Discuss these questions with your classmates.

1. What do you notice when you meet someone for the first time?

2. How important do you think first impressions are? Why?

3. Look at the photo. What do you think of this person from just looking at her? Do you think your first impression is accurate? Why or why not?

B. Listen to *The Q Classroom* online. Then answer these questions.

1. What accurate first impression did Yuna have?

2. What do Marcus and Sophy say are ways that people can give incorrect first impressions?

3. Do you agree with Felix's statement? Why or why not?

iQ PRACTICE Go to the online discussion board to discuss the Unit Question with your classmates. *Practice > Unit 1 > Activity 1*

UNIT OBJECTIVE

Listen to a lecture and an excerpt from a radio show and gather information and ideas to give a short talk about an accurate first impression.

A good way to remember a lecture is to put the key ideas into your own words. This will also help you confirm that you understood all the information and that your notes are complete.

As soon as possible after a lecture, put the key, or most important, ideas into your own words, and say them out loud to a study partner or to yourself. Saying them out loud will help you clarify the ideas and remember them better.

Imagine this situation: Your friend had to miss class because he was ill. The next day, he asks you to tell him about the lecture. What would you tell him?

You would probably give him the following information:

- the topic of the lecture

- the main ideas

- a few important points and examples

This is the same information that you use when you summarize. A **summary** is a shorter version of the information that includes all of the main ideas, but only a few details.

Here are some phrases that are used as signposts.

The professor talked about . . .

She explained . . .

She told us . . .

Then he discussed . . .

He gave us the example of . . .

After that he wrapped up with . . .

A. IDENTIFY Listen to an excerpt from a lecture on first impressions. Then discuss the questions with a partner.

1. What is the topic?

2. What two main points does the speaker make?

3. What is one detail that illustrates each main point?

B. RESTATE With a partner, take turns summarizing the lecture excerpt.

iQ PRACTICE Go online for more practice using notes to summarize a lecture. *Practice > Unit 1 > Activity 2*

LISTENING 1

OBJECTIVE ▶

The Psychology of First Impressions

You are going to listen to a lecture about first impressions. As you listen to the lecture, gather information and ideas about first impressions.

PREVIEW THE LISTENING

TIP FOR SUCCESS

Presentations and talks often begin with a short story or anecdote. The story is usually an example of the topic the speaker is going to talk about.

A. PREVIEW A psychologist will explain how first impressions affect our opinion of a new person. Check (✓) the statement about first impressions you think is true.

☐ First impressions give us a good idea of what a person is really like.

☐ We often make errors because of first impressions.

ACADEMIC LANGUAGE

Positive and *negative* are among the 600 most common spoken academic words, but *positive* is used more frequently than *negative*.

⎯⎯⎯⎯⎯ **OPAL**
Oxford Phrasal Academic Lexicon

B. VOCABULARY Read aloud these words from Listening 1. Check (✓) the ones you know. Use a dictionary to define any new or unknown words. Then discuss with a partner how the words will relate to the unit.

assume *(v.)* 🔑 OPAL	**form an impression** *(v. phr.)*
behavior *(n.)* OPAL	**negative** *(adj.)* 🔑 OPAL
briefly *(adv.)* OPAL	**positive** *(adj.)* 🔑 OPAL
encounter *(n.)* OPAL	**sample** *(n.)* 🔑 OPAL
error *(n.)* 🔑 OPAL	**trait** *(n.)*

🔑 Oxford 3000™ words   **OPAL** Oxford Phrasal Academic Lexicon

iQ PRACTICE Go online to listen and practice your pronunciation.
Practice > Unit 1 > Activity 3

WORK WITH THE LISTENING

A. LISTEN AND TAKE NOTES Listen to the lecture about first impressions. Before you listen, look at the outline below. As you listen, add the topic and important details.

iQ RESOURCES Go online to download extra vocabulary support.
Resources > Extra Vocabulary > Unit 1

Topic: _____ *How we form first impression* _____

Example: Waiting in line at a coffee shop

Main idea: Impressions of others

Detail(s)

First mistake: _____

Second mistake: _____

Main idea: When we view our own behavior

Detail: It's not our personality; it's the _____.

B. RESTATE Work with a partner. Take turns using your notes to summarize the lecture.

C. CATEGORIZE Read the statements. Write *T* (true) or *F* (false). Then correct each false statement to make it true.

1. __F__ First impressions tell the ~~whole~~ story.   *only part of*

2. ____ If a person is happy when we meet her, we will often think she is happy all the time.

3. ____ Our first impressions give us an accurate picture of the whole person.

4. ____ We judge other people's behavior differently from our own.

D. IDENTIFY Read the statements. Then listen again. Circle the answer or answers that best complete each statement.

1. People _____ what they see in a first encounter.

   a. often make mistakes about

   b. make sense of information from

   c. form very accurate impressions from

2. People assume that their first impressions tell them about
_____ person.

   a. a sample of a

   b. most of a

   c. the whole

3. If we think a person is happy when we first meet her, we will think she
is also _____.

   a. friendly

   b. boring

   c. kind

4. If someone else does something negative, we think _____.

   a. it is because of his personality

   b. he is a bad person

   c. it is because of how he felt that day

5. If we do something negative, we think it is because of _____.

   a. our personality

   b. the situation

   c. someone else

E. **EVALUATE** Check (✓) the statements you think the lecturer agrees
with. Discuss your answers with a partner. Support your arguments with
information from the lecture.

   ☐ 1. If a stranger behaves rudely, you may assume he isn't intelligent.

   ☐ 2. First impressions are rarely accurate.

   ☐ 3. People make more excuses for their own bad behavior.

   ☐ 4. An example of behavior can tell us a lot about someone's personality.

F. DISCUSS Read the text below. Discuss the questions with a partner.

On my first day of college, I was moving into my dorm room when my roommate, Renee, came in. She had already moved in and taken the bed by the window. Her stuff was everywhere. Her parents were with her. They were very nice and introduced themselves, but Renee was quiet and didn't really look at me. I didn't say much either because I thought she didn't like me. She threw her bag on her bed and they all left. I was very upset. I thought Renee was rude and mean. I was mad that she didn't even give me a chance.

An hour or so later, Renee came back to the room. She apologized for her rudeness. She had just had a bad argument with her parents and was upset with them. She described their fight in a very funny way, and we both laughed. After that, she became one of my best friends. She's the perfect roommate.

1. How accurate was the writer's first impression of her roommate?
   The writers thought Renee was rude and mean the is interesting
2. How does this story illustrate the points the speaker made in her lecture?
   Speaker first told her first imp and then speaker talked about her real person

TIP FOR SUCCESS
Pay attention to articles. They come before nouns and help you identify parts of speech.

G. VOCABULARY Use the new vocabulary from Listening 1. Complete each sentence with the correct word or phrase.

assume (v.)	error (n.)	positive (adj.)
behavior (n.)	form an impression (v. phr.)	sample (n.)
briefly (adv.)	negative (adj.)	trait (n.)
encounter (n.)		

1. I took a(n) _____ sample _____ of the carpet home to see whether I liked the color in my living room.

2. Alberto made several _____ error _____ on his math test because he didn't study hard enough.

3. Luisa said she wasn't feeling well, so I _____ assume _____ she's not going out tonight.

4. The teacher went over yesterday's assignment very _____ briefly _____. We only spent about fifteen minutes on it, so I still have some questions.

5. When I meet new people, I watch their _____ behavior _____ closely to see what they are like.

6. It only takes a few minutes to _____ f a l _____ of someone you meet for the first time.

7. One _____ negative _____ thing about moving to a new place is leaving your friends and family behind.

8. Most of my good friends have one personality _____ trait _____ in common—they are all very funny.

9. Do you usually have a(n) ___positive___ feeling about people when you meet them for the first time? I do because I think most people are good.

10. My first ___encounter___ with my new neighbors was very unpleasant. We argued about the amount of noise they were making.

iQ PRACTICE Go online for more practice with the vocabulary.
Practice > Unit 1 > Activity 4

iQ PRACTICE Go online for additional listening and comprehension.
Practice > Unit 1 > Activity 5

The first imp might be wrong

 # SAY WHAT YOU THINK

DISCUSS Discuss the questions in a group.

1. In this lecture, the speaker says we often think that the way a person behaves when we first meet him is the way he behaves all the time. From your personal experience, do you agree or disagree? Give examples.

2. Have you ever formed a first impression of someone that was wrong? Explain.

LISTENING SKILL Making inferences

Making inferences means to draw conclusions about information that is not stated directly by using information that you already know or that is stated directly. Making inferences while listening can help deepen your understanding of what you hear.

Listen to a student talking about meeting his professor for the first time.

> When I first met my professor, he shook my hand firmly and then asked me questions about myself. He was very polite. He also was relaxed and seemed interested in what I was saying.

Even though the student does not state directly that his first impression of his professor was positive, you can infer or conclude that he did from the information he does state directly.

- He shook my hand firmly.
- He asked questions.
- He was relaxed and seemed interested.

iQ RESOURCES Go online to watch the Listening Skill Video.
Resources > Video > Unit 1 > Listening Skill Video

A. EXPLAIN Listen to a student talk about a first impression. Take notes as you listen. Then answer the questions.

1. Do you think it was a positive or negative first impression? Why? What information from your notes helped you answer?

2. Do you think the speaker likes Lee? Why? What information from your notes helped you answer?

B. DISCUSS Work with a partner. Compare your answers.

C. EVALUATE Listen to the speaker's opinion of Lee. Take notes as you listen. Compare what the speaker says about Lee with your answers in Activity A.

D. CREATE Work with a partner. Tell a story about meeting someone for the first time. Describe what she or he did and a few things you noticed. Don't say how you felt about the person. Ask your partner to infer whether your impression was positive or negative.

iQ PRACTICE Go online for more practice making inferences.
Practice > Unit 1 > Activity 6

A Review of Books about First Impressions

You are going to listen to an excerpt of a radio program with someone who reviews books. She and the host talk about two books that deal with first impressions and quick thinking. As you listen, gather information and ideas about the accuracy of first impressions.

PREVIEW THE LISTENING

A. PREVIEW Look at the black lines at the left. Which one is longer? How do you know?

B. VOCABULARY Read aloud these words from Listening 2. Check (✓) the ones you know. Use a dictionary to define any new or unknown words. Then discuss with a partner how the words will relate to the unit.

assess *(v.)* ♎ OPAL	**expert** *(n.)* ♎ OPAL
association *(n.)* ♎ OPAL	**familiar** *(adj.)* ♎ OPAL
concentrate *(v.)* ♎ OPAL	**observation** *(n.)* ♎ OPAL
conscious *(adj.)* ♎	**reaction** *(n.)* ♎ OPAL
effective *(adj.)* ♎ OPAL	**reliable** *(adj.)* ♎ OPAL

♎ Oxford 3000™ words   **OPAL** Oxford Phrasal Academic Lexicon

iQ PRACTICE   Go online to listen and practice your pronunciation.
Practice > Unit 1 > Activity 8

WORK WITH THE LISTENING

A. LISTEN AND TAKE NOTES Listen to the book discussion. Before you listen, look at the partial outline below. As you listen, take notes on the main ideas, examples, and other details. After the listening is over, go back and add to or edit your notes for clarity.

iQ RESOURCES Go online to download extra vocabulary support.
Resources > Extra Vocabulary > Unit 1

Topic: Books on first impressions

Main Idea: Both writers think first impressions can be _____*accurate*_____,

but there are some ___*problem*_____ *mistake*_____.

Malcolm Gladwell wrote _____*blink*_____.

We use __*observations*___ of a thin slice of behavior to make ___*judgments*___

of people. Instinctive reaction is often _____*right*_____.

Example: Students are accurate in judging how _*effective*_ their *instructors* are.

Daniel Kahneman wrote _____*thinking fast and slow*_____.

Two systems:

System 1: _____*fast*_____, always __*assess*__ *assesign*___, without conscious thought

Example 1: __*you might walk around the ?*_____

Example 2: _*people might think old when they see slow*_

System 2: slow, use when we _____, need to *concentrate*. *and gry*

System 1 forms ___*first impression*___ but System 2 helps with __*accuracy*_.

Problems with ___*fast thinking*_____:

What you see is ____*all there is*_____.

Trust something that is ____*good behavior*____ *familiar*____.

Trust a message that is ____*familiar. gray and yellow.* *good font color*

Experts: usually have *at least 10 000*_____ hours of practice, often able to

____*form accurate first impression.*_____

B. RESTATE With a partner, take turns summarizing the discussion from your notes.

Malcolm Gladwell

Daniel Kahneman

CRITICAL THINKING STRATEGY

Comparing and contrasting

To **compare** means to find ways that things are the same. To **contrast** means to find ways that they are different. Comparing and contrasting helps you deepen your understanding of the things you are investigating.

To compare, ask yourself, *How are these things the same?* To contrast, ask yourself, *How are these things different?* Thinking this way can help you make connections between the things you are comparing and contrasting.

iQ PRACTICE Go online to watch the Critical Thinking Video and check your comprehension. *Practice > Unit 1 > Activity 7*

C. **ANALYZE** Complete the chart with ideas that compare and contrast Malcolm Gladwell's ideas with Daniel Kahneman's. Add at least two details to each side of the chart.

Compare	Contrast

D. ANALYZE Complete the chart with information from the listening. Listen again if needed.

	System 1	System 2
Speed	fast	slow
Example	walk around ladder	solve math problem
Accuracy	may have problems	helps with accuracy
Problems	what	tired
What helps it work better	practice	sleep, food

E. IDENTIFY Match the example with the idea it supports.

_d_ 1. Students' accurate first impressions   a. repetition of a false statement

_e_ 2. Predicting what will happen   b. slow, gray, old

_b_ _a_ 3. Association of ideas   c. someone who plays chess

_a_ _b_ 4. Trusting the familiar   d. effectiveness of instructors

_c_ 5. Experts with a lot of practice   e. a person on a ladder

F. CATEGORIZE Read the sentences. Then listen again and write *T* (true), *F* (false), or *DS* (doesn't say).

_DS_ 1. People use fast thinking more than slow thinking.

_F_ 2. It takes several minutes to form an accurate first impression of an instructor.

_F_ 3. System 1 checks on the accuracy of System 2.

_T_ _DS_ 4. We trust the color blue more than the color gray in messages.

_DS_ 5. Younger people are better at fast thinking than older people.
_DS_

G. APPLY Compare answers with a partner. Correct the false statements. If necessary, listen and check your answers.

H. DISCUSS Work with a group to discuss the questions.

1. According to Gladwell, our first impressions are often reliable. Do you think this is true? Why or why not?   actual

2. According to Kahneman, we use fast thinking more than slow thinking. When do you use each kind of thinking?

3. Kahneman says we trust people and messages sometimes when we shouldn't. Do you agree that this is a problem? Explain.

I. **SYNTHESIZE** Read more information below on first impressions from two researchers. With a partner, list and discuss five tips you can give others about making first impressions. Use this information and the information from *Blink*.

Nalini Ambady was a researcher at Tufts University. She did a study on how well students could make judgments about instructors from a short video. According to Ambady, when people think more before making a decision, the decisions tend not to be as good as when they make them without thinking.

Frank Bernieri of Oregon State University says that research suggests that people who are more confident about their judgments of people are actually less accurate. He advises people to try to convince themselves of the opposite point of view. For example, if you assume someone is rude and unkind, you should try to see his or her behavior in a completely different way.

Tips:

1. _____

2. _____

3. _____

4. _____

5. _____

J. VOCABULARY Use the new vocabulary from Listening 2. Read the sentences. Circle the answer that best matches the meaning of each bold word.

1. I make a **conscious** effort to stay in regular contact with all my friends. I make time to call and email them often.

   a. accidental   b. intentional   c. occasional

2. Watching a video is an **effective** way to study someone's behavior. You can learn a lot from the way people move their hands.

   a. successful   b. interesting   c. unusual

3. Marcos is an **expert** at swimming. He has been doing it a long time.

   a. beginner   b. failure   c. skillful person

4. Police officers often have to **assess** a dangerous situation quickly.

   a. describe   b. change   c. judge

5. My car isn't **reliable**. There is always something wrong with it.

   a. dependable   b. expensive   c. comfortable

6. I think I've seen that man before. He looks very **familiar**.

   a. attractive   b. well known   c. happy

7. After hours of **observation**, the researchers reached three main conclusions about the animal's behavior.

   a. listening   b. watching   c. talking

8. A lot of people make an **association** between being confident and being effective.

   a. mental connection   b. emotional connection   c. physical connection

9. Please don't talk to me while I do this assignment. I can't **concentrate**.

   a. hear   b. speak   c. pay attention

10. I thought he might be upset, so his excited **reaction** surprised me.

   a. awareness   b. response   c. presentation

iQ PRACTICE Go online for more practice with the vocabulary.
Practice > Unit 1 > Activity 9

WORK WITH THE VIDEO

A. PREVIEW Have you ever made a bad impression in an important situation? What happened?

VIDEO VOCABULARY

blow one's chances (*v. phr.*) to waste an opportunity to succeed

outrageous (*adj.*) very strange or unusual

mind-boggling (*adj.*) difficult to imagine, understand, or believe

err (*v.*) to make mistakes

conservative (*adj.*) traditional

air a grievance (*v. phr.*) to tell people that you think something is unfair; to complain

iQ RESOURCES Go online to watch the video about mistakes in job interviews.
Resources > Video > Unit 1 > Unit Video

B. CATEGORIZE Watch the video two or three times. Take notes in the first part of the chart.

	Mistakes	Examples
Notes from the video		
My ideas		

C. EXTEND What other mistakes do people make in job interviews? Write your ideas in the chart above.

SAY WHAT YOU THINK

SYNTHESIZE Think about the unit video, Listening 1, and Listening 2 as you discuss the questions.

1. In what kinds of situations do you think first impressions are usually accurate?

2. In what ways are job interviews similar to other types of first impressions people make? How are they different?

VOCABULARY SKILL Suffixes

Use **suffixes** and other word endings to help you recognize parts of speech. Recognizing the part of speech will help you guess the meaning of an unfamiliar word. It will also help you expand your vocabulary as you notice other parts of speech in the same word family.

Common noun suffixes: *-acy, -er / -or, -ment, -ness, -tion, -ence / -ance, -ise*

☐ accur**acy**, research**er**, invent**or**, amuse**ment**, friendli**ness**, atten**tion**, confid**ence**

Common verb suffixes: *-ate, -en, -ize, -ify / fy*

☐ stimul**ate**, strength**en**, energ**ize**, ident**ify**

Common adjective suffixes: *-able, -al, -ful, -ive, -ous, -ic*

☐ depend**able**, tradition**al**, care**ful**, effect**ive**, humor**ous**, artist**ic**

Common adverb suffixes: *-ly, -ally*

☐ particular**ly**, univers**ally**

A. IDENTIFY Look at the new words. For each word, write the suffix, the part of speech, and the base word from which the new word is formed.

New word	Suffix	Part of speech	Base word
1. accuracy	-acy	noun	accurate
2. assumption	tion	noun	assume
3. consciously	ly	adverb	as conscious
4. reliable	able	adjective	rely
5. effectively	ly	adverb	effective
6. expertise	ise	noun	expert
7. concentration	ion	noun	concentrate

B. DISCUSS Work with a partner. Discuss the meanings of the new words from Activity A. Then use a dictionary to check the definitions of any words you are not sure of.

C. APPLY Complete each sentence with the correct word from Activity A.

1. Solving math problems often requires a lot of _____.

2. _____ is really important in grammar, so you should try not to make mistakes.

3. We often make _____ about people because of the way they look. Then we sometimes discover that our first impressions were incorrect.

4. That professor has written many books and is known for her ___expertise___ in social psychology.

5. If an advertisement is ___effectively___ designed, sales of the product will increase.

6. Jay is very ___reliable___. He always arrives on time for everything.

7. I have to make decisions very ___consciously___ when I go shopping. If I don't, I buy things I really don't need without even realizing it.

iQ PRACTICE Go online for more practice with suffixes.
Practice > Unit 1 > Activity 10

SPEAKING

At the end of this unit, you will give a short talk to a partner about a first impression. Make sure to take conversational turns when you talk to your partner.

GRAMMAR Auxiliary verbs *do, be, have*

The **auxiliary verbs** *do*, *be*, and *have* are used to make questions and negative statements.

Use *do* with the simple present and simple past.

Simple present	**Simple past**
Does he like pizza?	**Did** they bring their books?
He **doesn't** like pizza.	They **didn't** bring their books.

Use *be* with the present and past continuous.

Present continuous	**Past continuous**
Are you reading?	**Was** Mr. Knight teaching here last year?
We **aren't** reading now.	He **wasn't** teaching here last year.

Use *have* with the present perfect.

Present perfect

Has she left yet?
Nancy **hasn't** left yet.

A. COMPOSE Rewrite the sentences as negative statements. Use the correct form of *do*, *be*, or *have* as the auxiliary verb.

1. I have to concentrate very hard when I'm driving.
   don't
2. Bill thinks first impressions about teachers are usually accurate.
   not
3. Sara assumed the ad was true.
   doesn't   didn't   wasn't
4. Waleed is nervous about giving his presentation next week.
   isn't
5. I've formed a positive impression of that company.
   haven't

B. COMPOSE Rewrite the sentences as questions. Use the correct form of *do*, *be*, or *have* as the auxiliary verb.

1. You have made incorrect assumptions because of how someone looked.
   Have you made
2. You like talking to new people on the phone.
   Do you like
3. Hatem made lots of friends at school.
   Did Hatem make
4. The experts were able to assess the situation more quickly.
   Were the experts
5. Jamal has created an effective message about the product.
   Has Jamal

C. EXTEND Work with a partner. Take turns asking and answering the questions from Activity B. Use auxiliary verbs in your short answers.

A: *Do you like talking to new people on the phone?*
B: *Yes, I do./No, I don't.*

iQ PRACTICE Go online for more practice with auxiliary verbs.
Practice > Unit 1 > Activities 11–12

PRONUNCIATION Contractions with auxiliary verbs

Auxiliary verbs are usually unstressed and can be shortened as part of a **contraction**. Most contractions can be used in speech and informal writing, but some are only used in speech.

Listen to these examples of contractions.

Contractions used in speech or writing

> She**'s** eating now. (She is eating now.)
> They**'re** watching TV. (They are watching TV.)
> Lisa**'s** already left. (Lisa has already left.)
> We**'ve** finished our work. (We have finished our work.)

Contractions used only in speech

> What**'s** it cost? (What does it cost?)
> Where**'d** you go? (Where did you go?)
> Why**'d** he arrive so late? (Why did he arrive so late?)

 A. APPLY Listen to these sentences with contractions. Write the full form of the auxiliary verb.

1. Who _____ *is* _____ your favorite author?

2. Where _____ ~~*is*~~ ~~*do*~~*did* _____ you go on your last vacation?

3. Mary _____ *is* _____ going to the store.

4. We _____ *have* _____ usually eaten by 6:00.

5. What _____ ~~*are*~~ ~~*do*~~ *did* _____ you do after class yesterday?

6. The girls _____ *have* _____ been here before.

B. RESTATE Work with a partner. Take turns saying the sentences from Activity A. Use the full form of the auxiliary verbs. Then practice saying them with contractions.

iQ PRACTICE Go online for more practice with contractions with auxiliary verbs. *Practice > Unit 1 > Activity 13*

When you are speaking with someone, it is polite to take turns talking. Taking turns keeps the conversation going and shows that you are interested in what the other person is saying.

If the other person asks you a question, answer it, and add some new information. If possible, ask a question of your own. Here are some questions you can use.

What do you think?   How about you?

Do you agree?   You know?

Right?   OK?

A. IDENTIFY Complete the conversation with questions from the Speaking Skill box. Then practice the conversation with a partner.

Tony: Hi. I'm Tony. It's nice to meet you.

Alex: My name's Alex. Nice to meet you, too. Are you a new student?

Tony: No. I've been studying here for two years.
_____What do you think?_____How about you?____
1

Alex: I just started this week, but so far this class looks interesting.
_____Do you agree?_____
2

Tony: I agree. The teacher's very effective. The book he's using looks good, too.
_____Right?_____
3

Alex: Yeah. He seems friendly and interesting.

B. CREATE Read the questions and take notes to help you answer them. Then have a conversation about each question with a partner. Keep the conversations going for at least three turns each, and signal your partner's turn by using questions from the Speaking Skill box.

1. Who was your most effective teacher when you were a child? What impressed you about him or her?

2. Have you ever made a bad first impression on someone else? What did you do?

iQ PRACTICE Go online for more practice with taking conversational turns. *Practice > Unit 1 > Activity 14*

UNIT ASSIGNMENT   Give a short talk

OBJECTIVE ▶

In this assignment, you are going to give a talk to a partner about a first impression. As you prepare your talk, think about the Unit Question, "Are first impressions accurate?" Use information from Listening 1, Listening 2, the unit video, and your work in this unit to support your talk. Refer to the Self-Assessment checklist on page 24.

CONSIDER THE IDEAS

CATEGORIZE Which items in the chart tell you the most about new people when you are forming a first impression? Check (✓) whether you think each item is very important, important, or not important. Then compare and discuss your answers with a partner.

	Very important	Important	Not important
their level of politeness	☑	☐	☑
their clothing	☐	☑	☑
their hairstyle	☐	☐	☑
their voice	☐	☐	☑
their eye contact	☑	☐	☐
their attitude to money	☐	☐	☑
the way they drive	☑	☐	☐
their job	☐	☐	☑
their likes and dislikes	☑	☐	☐
Your own ideas:			
	☐	☐	☐
	☐	☐	☐

PREPARE AND SPEAK

A. GATHER IDEAS Complete these steps.

1. Think about a time when your first impression of someone was incorrect.

2. Brainstorm as much as you can remember about the situation.

3. Then write what you thought about the person when you first met and how your first impression was wrong.

B. ORGANIZE IDEAS Use your ideas from Activity A to help you answer these questions. Do not write full sentences. Just write notes to help you remember your answers.

Who was the person? _____

Where, when, and why did you meet? _____

What was your first impression? Why? _____

When did you realize your first impression was wrong? _____

What changed your mind? _____

What do you think about the person now? _____

C. SPEAK Tell your partner about your first impression of the person you chose. Refer to the Self-Assessment checklist below before you begin.

1. Explain why you formed that impression and why you were wrong.

2. You can refer to your notes, but do not read exactly what you wrote.

3. Talk for at least one minute.

iQ PRACTICE   Go online for your alternate Unit Assignment.
Practice > Unit 1 > Activity 15

CHECK AND REFLECT

A. CHECK Think about the Unit Assignment as you complete the Self-Assessment checklist.

SELF-ASSESSMENT	Yes	No
I was able to speak easily about the topic.	☐	☐
My partner understood me.	☐	☐
I used vocabulary from the unit.	☐	☐
I used auxiliary verbs and contractions.	☐	☐
I took turns when speaking.	☐	☐

B. REFLECT Discuss these questions with a partner or group.

1. What is something new you learned in this unit?

2. Look back at the Unit Question—Are first impressions accurate? Is your answer different now than when you started this unit? If yes, how is it different? Why?

iQ PRACTICE   Go to the online discussion board to discuss the questions.
Practice > Unit 1 > Activity 16

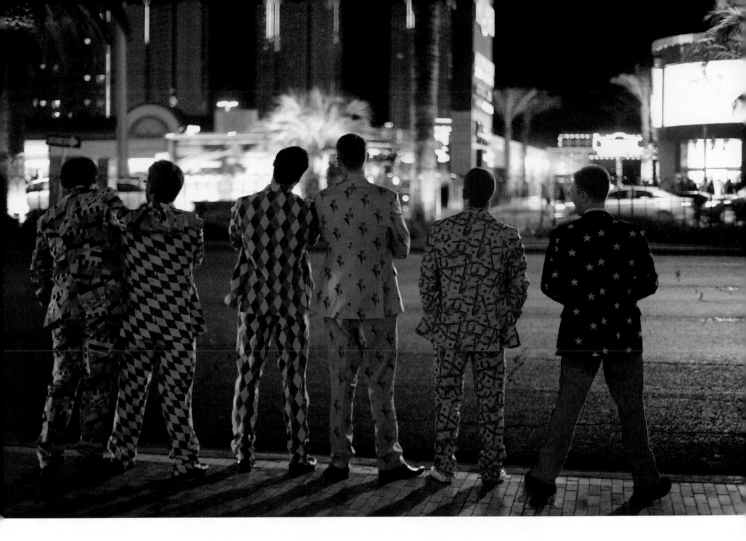

TRACK YOUR SUCCESS

iQ PRACTICE Go online to check the words and phrases you have learned in this unit. *Practice > Unit 1 > Activity 17*

Check (✓) the skills you learned. If you need more work on a skill, refer to the page(s) in parentheses.

NOTE-TAKING ☐ I can use my notes to summarize a lecture. (p. 4)

LISTENING ☐ I can make inferences. (p. 9)

CRITICAL THINKING ☐ I can compare and contrast two things. (p. 13)

VOCABULARY ☐ I can use suffixes. (p. 18)

GRAMMAR ☐ I can use the auxiliary verbs *do*, *be*, and *have*. (p. 20)

PRONUNCIATION ☐ I can use contractions with auxiliary verbs. (p. 21)

SPEAKING ☐ I can take conversational turns. (p. 22)

OBJECTIVE ▶ ☐ I can gather information and ideas to give a short talk about an accurate first impression.

Nutritional Science

2

CRITICAL THINKING	predicting topics or ideas
LISTENING	listening for causes and effects
NOTE-TAKING	taking notes on causes and effects
VOCABULARY	adjective-noun collocations
GRAMMAR	quantifiers with count and noncount nouns
PRONUNCIATION	links with /j/ and /w/
SPEAKING	giving advice

Why do we change the foods we eat?

A. Discuss these questions with your classmates.

1. Do you think that it's common for people to change the kinds of food they eat? Why or why not?

2. What reasons do people sometimes have for changing the types of food they eat?

3. Look at the photo. What does the food in this kitchen tell you about the people's tastes and their way of life?

B. Listen to *The Q Classroom* online. Then match the ideas in the box with the students.

a. ~~To help protect the natural environment~~
b. To be healthier
c. To adapt to a different culture
d. To be better at sports

Some reasons for changing what we eat	
Sophy	a. To help protect the natural environment
Felix	d
Marcus	b
Yuna	c

iQ PRACTICE Go to the online discussion board to discuss the Unit Question with your classmates. *Practice > Unit 2 > Activity 1*

UNIT OBJECTIVE

Watch a video and listen to a class discussion. Then listen to a lecture. Gather information and ideas to conduct a class survey on food preferences.

LISTENING 1

A Billion Pounds of Spices

OBJECTIVE ▶

You are going to watch a US news report about international spices. Then you will listen to part of a class discussion about the video. As you watch and listen, gather ideas about why people change the foods they eat.

VIDEO

PREVIEW THE LISTENING

CRITICAL THINKING STRATEGY

Predicting topics or ideas

When you preview a listening passage, you naturally take guesses about what you might hear. Taking such guesses is called **predicting**.

Before listening, look at all of the information available to you, such as the title of the listening, any blurb or short description about it, its source (where it comes from), and/or any supporting images. Consider what you already know about:

- the general topic—as deduced from the title, description, or images
- the speaker(s)—if they are introduced ahead of time
- the context—such as a television program, a classroom discussion, etc.

Use all of that information to make predictions about what you might hear.

For example, imagine that you are listening to an interview that starts, "Today we are going to talk about health and dairy foods—milk, cheese, yogurt, and so on. Our guest today is Doctor Alissa Barton from Eastern Hospital."

From the announcement of the topic, you could predict that the topics of calories and fat might come up, because you know that some people drink low-fat milk.

Because the guest is a doctor at a hospital, you might also predict the topic of serious health problems might come up.

iQ PRACTICE Go online to watch the Critical Thinking Video and check your comprehension. *Practice > Unit 2 > Activity 2*

A. PREDICT Look at the title of Listening 1 and the picture, and re-read the description next to the unit objective. What do you think Listening 1 is going to be about? Make predictions with a partner. Discuss what you already know about the following:

1. the general topic
2. the speakers
3. the context

B. PREVIEW Look at the list of spices that will be mentioned in the video and the class discussion. Check (✓) each spice that you are familiar with. Compare your list with a partner's.

- ☐ Aleppo pepper
- ☐ allspice
- ☐ basil
- ☐ black onion seed
- ☐ cayenne pepper
- ☐ cinnamon
- ☐ cumin
- ☐ ginger
- ☐ paprika
- ☐ (black) pepper
- ☐ oregano
- ☐ salt
- ☐ turmeric
- ☐ wattle seed
- ☐ za'atar

ACADEMIC LANGUAGE

The corpus shows that *with respect to* is often used in academic speaking to show the relationship between ideas.

⎯⎯⎯⎯⎯⎯ OPAL
Oxford Phrasal Academic Lexicon

C. VOCABULARY Read aloud these words from Listening 1. Check (✓) the ones you know. Use a dictionary to define any new or unknown words. Then discuss with a partner how the words will relate to the unit.

burn *(v.)* 🔑	**local** *(adj.)* 🔑 OPAL
consume *(v.)* 🔑 OPAL	**rare** *(adj.)* 🔑
ethnic *(adj.)* OPAL	**season** *(v.)* 🔑
experiment *(v.)* 🔑 OPAL	**spicy** *(adj.)* 🔑
key *(adj.)* 🔑 OPAL	**with respect to** *(prep. phr.)* OPAL

🔑 Oxford 3000™ words   OPAL Oxford Phrasal Academic Lexicon

iQ PRACTICE Go online to listen and practice your pronunciation.
Practice > Unit 2 > Activity 3

WORK WITH THE LISTENING

iQ RESOURCES Go online to watch the video.
Resources > Video > Unit 2 > Listening 1 Part 1

A LISTEN AND TAKE NOTES Watch the video.* Then listen to the class discussion. Use the left column of the chart to list some of the spices the speakers mention. Use the right column to take notes about each spice. Then compare charts with a partner.

iQ RESOURCES Go online to download extra vocabulary support.
Resources > Extra Vocabulary > Unit 2

salt

Spices	Details

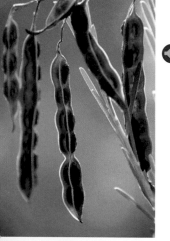

wattle seed

B. IDENTIFY Watch the video and listen to the class discussion again. Match each spice with the best description, according to the video and discussion. Use your notes to help you.

____ 1. Aleppo pepper

____ 2. ginger

____ 3. oregano

____ 4. paprika

____ 5. salt

____ 6. turmeric

____ 7. wattle seed

____ 8. za'atar

a. seasoning often used in Lebanese cooking

b. used to make curry

c. tangy and not as hot as cayenne pepper

d. use has grown more than 50 percent

e. an Australian spice

f. a very old and common seasoning, often used with pepper

g. commonly used in Italian cooking

h. use has doubled in a five-year period

C. IDENTIFY Read the sentences. Circle the answer that best completes each statement. Use your notes to help you.

1. The "air is thick with exotic aromas" means that there are a lot of different _____ outside of the spice factory.

a. tastes

b. smells

c. sounds

turmeric

Audio version available. Resources > Audio > Unit 2

2. The narrator says the "melting pot" is responsible for increasing the number of spices Americans use. In this video, the phrase "melting pot" means: _____.

   a. diversity of people in the culture

   b. number of people in the culture

   c. cooking tools used in the culture

3. In the testing center, _____ disguises the color of the sample for professional tasters.

   a. software

   b. a mirror

   c. special lighting

4. The teacher says, "It's hard to draw a little box around a few dishes and say, 'This is local food.'" In this discussion, "draw a little box around" something means: _____.

   a. put it in a package so it can be carried

   b. say good things about it to advertise it

   c. separate it into a special group or category

5. According to the teacher's survey of the class, this spice has been used for a long time in the local area: _____.

   a. salt

   b. wattle seed

   c. turmeric

6. One student mentions that South Asian food is becoming more popular in their area as a way to explain why _____.

   a. another student's family has used turmeric for a long time

   b. no one in the class knew what turmeric is

   c. turmeric is a new spice in their area

7. The teacher says that claims about the healthiness of certain spices _____.

   a. have not been tested by scientific research

   b. can cause the spices to become more popular

   c. are almost always false and possibly dangerous

D. CATEGORIZE Read the statements. Write *T* (true) or *F* (false). Then explain your answers to a partner, using the information from Listening 1 for support.

_____ 1. The average American household has about four times as many types of spices as it had in the 1950s.

_____ 2. Because Americans are trying new spices, the McCormick Spice Company has lost business.

_____ 3. A family that eats "burgers, pizza, chicken, spaghetti, tacos, chili" has a diet drawn from many different countries.

_____ 4. The students in the discussion had eaten wattle seed before, but they thought it was called "turmeric."

_____ 5. The teacher believes strongly that eating turmeric improves one's health.

E. VOCABULARY Use the new vocabulary from Listening 1. Complete each sentence with the correct word or phrase.

---

burn *(v.)*   ethnic *(adj.)*   key *(adj.)*   rare *(adj.)*   spicy *(adj.)*
consume *(v.)*   experiment *(v.)*   local *(adj.)*   season *(v.)*   with respect to *(prep. phr.)*

---

1. I like most Lebanese food, but I don't have an opinion _____ za'atar because I've never tried it.

2. The people in this neighborhood are from many different _____ backgrounds, such as Polish, Irish, Somali, and Korean.

3. Of all the things we discussed today, the _____ idea to remember is that food shapes culture as much as culture shapes food.

4. Cooks often _____ tomato sauce with onions, basil, oregano, or other flavorings that soften the tang of the tomatoes.

5. The spice saffron is very expensive because it is very _____. Almost all of the world's supply comes from only one source—northeastern Iran—and it comes from a flower that blooms for only three weeks a year.

6. The winner of the apple-eating contest _____ 36 apples in five minutes.

7. A dish called *kifo*, made with raw beef, was once a _____ favorite, found only in part of southern Ethiopia. However, now it is popular throughout the country.

8. When a restaurant asks me if I want my food to be very _____, I always say yes. I like my food as hot as possible.

9. I like to _____ with different ingredients. I often buy new fruits and vegetables to try at home.

10. Sip the coffee first to make sure it's not too hot. Otherwise, you might _____ your tongue.

iQ PRACTICE Go online for more practice with the vocabulary.
Practice > Unit 2 > Activity 4

iQ PRACTICE Go online for additional listening and comprehension.
Practice > Unit 2 > Activity 5

SAY WHAT YOU THINK

DISCUSS Discuss the questions in a group.

1. Think about the people you know. Do you think their tastes in food are becoming more international? Give examples.

2. Do you agree with the teacher in the class discussion that the meaning of the term "local food" is always changing? Explain.

LISTENING SKILL Listening for causes and effects

Speakers often talk about **causes** and **effects** to help explain their opinions. Listening for the linking words and phrases that connect causes (reasons) and effects (results) will help you understand a speaker's main points.

Here are some words and phrases (in bold) that signal causes and effects.

I rarely cook **because** I'm tired when I get home.
    effect   cause

We usually eat at home **since** it's so expensive to eat out these days.
    effect   cause

Knowing people from other countries **leads to** a familiarity with new spices.
        cause   effect

The pasta tasted terrible, **so** we didn't eat it.
    cause   effect

Due to / Because of her healthy diet, Keiko lived to be 110 years old.
        cause   effect

Note: Use *due to* and *because of* before noun phrases. Use *because*, *since*, *as*, and *so* before clauses.

A. APPLY Listen to the sentences. Complete each sentence with the correct word or phrase.

1. _____Since_____ Judith Marcus was shopping for interesting spices, the reporter in the video talked to her.

2. Many people try to use less salt in their food _____because of_____ possible salt-related health problems.

3. _____Because_____ the student's family cooks Lebanese food, he is familiar with za'atar.

4. I like a lot of variety in my food, _____So_____ I am interested in trying some new spices.

B. IDENTIFY Listen to four statements from the video and class discussion. Complete the chart with the causes or effects you hear. Then circle the linking words. (Remember: You do not have to write every word you hear; try to write the important information or idea.)

Causes	Effects
1. Keeping track of changing tastes is a full-time job, →	(so) spice testers watch people's reactions
2. It's a somewhat rare Australian spice, →	it's so no familar anyone in this room
3. It's becoming a lot more popular →	because people here eat South Asian foods more
4. It's hard to draw a little box around a few dishes and say, "This is local food," →	Since the meaning of that is keeps changing too term

C. CREATE Think about your diet. How have your tastes changed over the years? For example, what foods do you eat now that you rejected as a child? What factors have caused your tastes to change? Make notes and share your ideas with a partner. Be sure to use linking words and phrases when giving causes and effects.

I don't eat really sweet foods anymore because they make me feel unwell. I have some friends who cook with peppers a lot, so I'm willing to eat hot peppers now.

[handwritten margin notes: mom cooks well, goes meat, green]

iQ PRACTICE Go online for more practice listening for causes and effects. *Practice > Unit 2 > Activity 6*

NOTE-TAKING SKILL Taking notes on causes and effects

When listening to identify causes and effects, you need to listen carefully for the key words and phrases that are used to introduce both causes and their effects.

To introduce a cause, you may hear: *as, because, because of, due to, since.*

To introduce an effect, you may hear: *as a result, consequently, so, therefore.* You may also hear a verb like *cause* or *lead to* before the effect.

To organize your notes, write *Cause* and *Effect* in a chart and note each piece of information in the appropriate column as you listen. Organizing your notes in this way will help you understand how ideas are related and help you review your notes.

A. IDENTIFY Listen to this section of a talk on nutrition. Check (✓) the words that introduce causes and effects.

☑ as	☑ because of	☐ since
☑ as a result	☐ consequently	☑ so
☐ because	☑ due to	☐ therefore

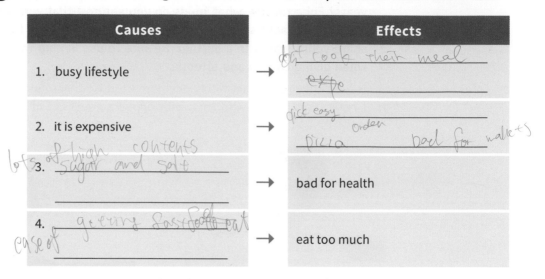

B. ANALYZE Listen again. Use this chart to complete each cause and effect.

Causes	Effects
1. busy lifestyle	→ dont cook their meal expe
2. it is expensive	→ dick easy order pizza bad for wallets
lots of high contents 3. sugar and salt	→ bad for health
4. greeing fasrfood eat case of	→ eat too much

iQ PRACTICE Go online for more practice taking notes on causes and effects. *Practice > Unit 2 > Activity 7*

LISTENING 2   A World of Food

OBJECTIVE ▶

You are going to listen to a lecture about healthy diets around the world. As you listen, gather information and ideas about why people change the foods they eat.

PREVIEW THE LISTENING

A. PREVIEW What makes one kind of diet healthier than another? Can you think of any cultures that have especially healthy diets?

B. VOCABULARY Read aloud these words from Listening 2. Check (✓) the ones you know. Use a dictionary to define any new or unknown words. Then discuss with a partner how the words will relate to the unit.

account for (v. phr.) 🔑 OPAL	**enjoy** (v.) 🔑
a function of (n. phr.) 🔑 OPAL	**feature** (n.) 🔑 OPAL
approximately (adv.) 🔑 OPAL	**illustrate** (v.) 🔑 OPAL
correlation (n.) OPAL	**play a role in** (v. phr.)
degree (n.) 🔑 OPAL	**risk** (n.) 🔑 OPAL

🔑 Oxford 3000™ words   **OPAL** Oxford Phrasal Academic Lexicon

iQ PRACTICE Go online to listen and practice your pronunciation.
Practice > Unit 2 > Activity 8

WORK WITH THE LISTENING

 A. LISTEN AND TAKE NOTES Listen to the lecture about exceptionally healthy diets. Before you listen, look at the chart below. As you listen, complete the causes and effects.

TIP FOR SUCCESS
Some cause-effect relationships are not introduced by key words like *because* or *so*. Listen to recognize both kinds—with key words and without.

iQ RESOURCES Go online to download extra vocabulary support.
Resources > Extra Vocabulary > Unit 2

Causes		Effects
following a super-diet (ex. Mediterranean, traditional Japanese diet)	→	much greater chance of living _a long healther life_
use oregano and thyme instead of _salt_	→	less likely to have _high pressure_
oil in fresh fish	→	reduce inflammation and _cancer_ risks
consuming _oll of oil_ instead of animal fats	→	_lower levels_ of "bad" cholesterol = better heart health
Japanese people eat smaller portions of food	→	can help with _weight cotrols → disease related_ _and minimize obesity_
Icelanders have about the same life expectancy as Italians	→	the Icelandic diet has _also attrated to attention_
super-diets have gotten attention	→	dietary changes around the _world_

Causes	Effects
people who eat super-diets also _hare long life_ →	stay _healthy_
they also enjoy close ties to others →	have lower psychological _____

 B. CATEGORIZE Read the statements. Listen to the lecture again. Write *T* (true) or *F* (false). Then correct each false statement to make it true.

_____ 1. Consuming a lot of salt is likely to lead to lower blood pressure.

_____ 2. Italians' life expectancy is more than a year longer than the life expectancy of people in the UK.

_____ 3. Fish is a much greater part of the diet for people in Japan than in Iceland.

_____ 4. Olive oil is a major part of the diet in the Mediterranean countries, Japan, and Iceland.

_____ 5. In the United States, the consumption of broccoli has increased much more than the population has.

_____ 6. The fact that two things occur together means that one of them causes the other.

C. IDENTIFY Listen again to the lecturer. Circle the answer that best completes each statement.

1. People who follow the Mediterranean diet and the traditional Japanese diet (live longer / are stronger) than other people.

2. Someone with (more / fewer) LDLs in the body has a better chance of having a healthy heart.

3. In approximately the last 20 years, the (production / consumption) of olive oil in the United States has increased by about 300 percent.

4. A long, healthy life probably (plays a role in / is a function of) many factors, including diet.

5. Having close ties to others in a village probably helps someone (stay fit / have less stress).

D. EVALUATE Read these summaries. Work with a partner to find two mistakes in each one. Correct the mistakes.

1. Outside the Mediterranean area, healthy diets can be found among the people of both Iceland and Japan. The traditional Icelandic diet is limited, and fish provides a lot of the protein for most Icelanders. Icelanders have the longest average lifespan in the world—85 years. The Japanese eat smaller portions of food, which may or may not lead to longer life in humans.

2. The Mediterranean diet probably leads to a much lower chance of living a long, healthy life. However, no one can prove that the Mediterranean diet directly leads to a long life. Using seasonings other than salt is good because it increases your blood pressure. Using olive oil instead of animal fats probably decreases your heart attack risk.

3. People around the world do not recognize the possible benefits of super-diets. The amount of broccoli consumed went up by about 300 percent in the U.S. and about 150 percent in Saudi Arabia in 20 years, possibly because of influence from the Mediterranean diet. But other factors like exercise and close ties to one's community are also important. Exercise probably helps a person stay healthy and fit. Close ties to a community can lead to harmful stress.

E. DISCUSS Discuss the questions in a group.

1. Do you think that diet is the main reason why some groups of people live exceptionally long? Explain.

2. Do you think it's possible for people in all areas of the world to achieve longer, healthier lives by copying certain elements of "super-diets"? Why or why not?

3. Have you ever made any changes to your diet in order to improve your health? Give one or two examples.

F. VOCABULARY Use the new vocabulary from Listening 2. Read the sentences. Circle the answer that best matches the meaning of each bold word or phrase.

1. My father stopped using so much salt. This probably **accounts for** his lower blood pressure.

   a. is a reason for   b. is a way of measuring   c. is a result of

2. The number of spices a culture uses is partly **a function of** the number of plants in the area.

   a. a description of   b. a way of using   c. a result of

3. A 65-year-old woman in this country can expect to live to **approximately** the age of 85.

   a. more than   b. about   c. only

4. You can judge people's **degree** of satisfaction with a dinner by how much they eat.

   a. training   b. level   c. problem

5. My generation **enjoys** a much healthier diet than our parents or grandparents did.

   a. has   b. hopes to have   c. claims to have

6. To **illustrate** his point, the professor displayed a graph with statistics relating to the increased consumption of olive oil in Saudi Arabia.

   a. demonstrate   b. write   c. research

7. Garlic—a strong-smelling relative of the onion—is an important **feature** of Italian, Korean, and Chinese cooking.

   a. benefit   b. characteristic   c. type

8. Some spices, such as salt, **play a role in** preserving food—that is, making the food last longer.

   a. are involved in   b. are wrongly used for   c. are not very good for

9. Scientists are conducting research to determine if there is a **correlation** between eating smaller amounts of food and living longer.

 a. disagreement   b. link   c. belief

10. People who eat too much of the spice nutmeg have a **risk** of feeling dizziness and stomach pains.

 a. certainty   b. opportunity   c. possible danger

iQ PRACTICE Go online for more practice with the vocabulary.
Practice > Unit 2 > Activity 9

? SAY WHAT YOU THINK

SYNTHESIZE Think about Listening 1 and Listening 2 as you discuss the questions.

1. What factors are most important in causing people to change their diets: health, a search for new experiences, a desire to be like others, or other factors?

2. To what extent might changes in diet threaten traditional cultures? Do cultures lose something when people depart from their traditional ways of eating?

VOCABULARY SKILL Adjective–noun collocations

Collocations are combinations of words that are often used together. For example, certain adjectives are often used with certain nouns. Using correct collocations will make your conversations sound more natural.

Here are some examples of adjective–noun collocations.

 When you eat before exercising, you should only have a **light meal**.
 There is nothing better than a **cold drink** on a hot summer day.
 I try not to eat too much **fast food**, but it's difficult because I love fries.
 Would you like cheesecake for dessert or just some **fresh fruit**?

A. APPLY Complete each collocation with a noun from the box.

diet   drink   food   snack   steak

1. a soft _____
2. junk _____
3. a juicy _____
4. a balanced _____
5. a quick _____

B. APPLY Complete each sentence with the correct collocation from Activity A.

1. Jim's favorite meal to cook at home is _____, served with potatoes.

2. To have _____, you need to eat lots of different kinds of healthy foods.

3. Do you want tea, or would you like _____ with lunch?

4. I used to eat chips and candy all the time. Now I hate _____!

5. I don't have time for a big lunch, so let's just have _____.

C. IDENTIFY Find and circle the adjective–noun collocation(s) in each sentence.

1. James has always had a very healthy appetite.

2. Generally, I try to avoid eating a lot of fatty foods.

3. There's nothing but deep-fried fish on this menu!

4. I like cooking, but I hate washing all the dirty dishes afterwards.

5. Regular exercise is an important part of staying healthy.

iQ PRACTICE Go online for more practice with adjective-noun collocations. *Practice ⟩ Unit 2 ⟩ Activity 10*

SPEAKING

OBJECTIVE ▶ At the end of this unit, you will interview three classmates about their favorite dishes. Make sure to give advice when you conduct your interviews.

GRAMMAR Quantifiers with count and noncount nouns

Count nouns are the names of things we can count, for example, one egg and two bananas. **Noncount nouns** are the names of things we cannot count, such as cheese and water.

How many / How much

Use *how many* with count nouns. Use *how much* with noncount nouns.

> **How many** apples do you eat a week?
> **How much** tea do you drink a day?

Too many / Too much

Use *too many / too much* when there is more than you want or need.

> You can have cookies once in a while, but don't eat **too many**.
> Don't drink **too much** coffee at bedtime, or you'll never fall asleep.

Enough / Not enough

Use *enough / not enough* with both count and noncount nouns.

> We have **enough** food for everybody.
> We don't have **enough** chairs.

iQ RESOURCES Go online to watch the Grammar Skill Video.
Resources > Video > Unit 2 > Grammar Skill Video

A. APPLY Complete the conversations with words and phrases from the box. Then practice the conversations with a partner.

enough	many	too many
not enough	much	too much

Eileen: Hey, that smells great. What are you cooking?

Debra: Chicken with chilies and rice. Do you want to try some?

Eileen: Sure . . . Wow! That's hot! How _____many_____ chilies did you put in?
1

Debra: Five. But they're really small. Don't you like spicy food?

Eileen: Yeah, I do, but it's too hot for me!

Anna: What do you think of the soup? It's potato and onion.

Susie: Hmm. It's OK. It seems like there is something missing, though.

Anna: Maybe I didn't put in _____enough_____ salt.
2

Susie: And it's pretty thick, isn't it?

Anna: Yes. I think I used _____too many_____ potatoes.
3

Muriel: How _____much_____ sugar did you put in this coffee?
4

Angela: One teaspoon.

Muriel: That's _____not enough_____ for me! I like my coffee very sweet.
5

Angela: Well, you shouldn't have _____too much_____. That's unhealthy.
6

TIP FOR SUCCESS

When listening, make sure you maintain eye contact. This encourages the speaker and shows that you are interested.

B. EXPLAIN Make a list of foods and drinks you like. Write *C* (count) or *N* (noncount) next to each item. Then discuss your favorite things to eat and drink with a partner. Be sure to use *much*, *many*, and *enough* correctly with count and noncount nouns.

Foods I like . . .   Drinks I like . . .

(C) eat enough Ramen.   (n) Drink much coke

(C) eat many pizzas.   (n) Drink enough cofee

(C) eat enough snacks   (n) Drink many bubble tea
                                                much

iQ PRACTICE Go online for more practice using quantifiers with count and noncount nouns. *Practice > Unit 2 > Activity 11*

iQ PRACTICE Go online for the Grammar Expansion: articles *a*, *an*, *the*, no article. *Practice > Unit 2 > Activity 12*

When certain words follow each other, additional sounds are created. These extra sounds make a natural **link** between the two words.

When a word beginning with a vowel follows a word that ends in the vowel sounds /i/, /eɪ/, or /aɪ/ (like *bee, say,* or *eye*), a /j/ sound is added between the words.

> I think Marco must **be** /j/ **Italian.**
> I can't see you tonight, but Tues**day** /j/ **is** fine.
> **I** /j/ **ate** salmon for dinner last night.

When a word beginning with a vowel follows a word that ends in the vowel sounds /u/, /o/, or /aʊ/ (like *who, no* and *how*), a /w/ sound is added between the words.

> Do **you** /w/ **eat** a balanced diet?
> Do you want to **go** /w/ **out** for lunch?
> **How** /w/ **is** your steak?

Pronouncing these linking sounds will help make your English sound more natural.

A. IDENTIFY Listen to the sentences. Write /j/ or /w/ in the correct places. Then listen again and check your answers.

1. We /j/ all eat things we know we shouldn't.

2. "Empty" calories have no nutritional value at all.

3. I can't drink coffee, but tea is fine.

4. Cheese has calcium, so it's good for your teeth.

5. Sometimes in the evening I'm too tired to cook.

6. Marie makes sure the cheese is ready to go out on sale.

7. The smell of a dish can be as important as its taste or appearance.

8. Enrique thinks people pay a lot for coffee so they want to enjoy it.

B. APPLY Listen again. Repeat each sentence. Practice linking /j/ and /w/.

iQ PRACTICE Go online for more practice using links with /j/ and /w/.
Practice > Unit 2 > Activity 13

The words *should*, *shouldn't*, and *ought to* are used to give advice. Listen to these sentences.

⌐ According to the teacher, we **should** remember that food customs change.
  He **shouldn't** drink a lot of soda.
⌐ They **ought to** eat more fish.

You can sound more polite by starting a sentence with *perhaps*.

⌐ **Perhaps** you **should** eat more fruit and vegetables.

You can give stronger advice by adding *really*.

⌐ You **really ought to** eat more fruit and vegetables.

A. DISCUSS Work with a partner. Discuss your eating and drinking habits. Take turns making true statements about your diet. After each of your partner's statements, give some advice, using *should / shouldn't* or *ought to*. Remember to use count and noncount nouns correctly.

A: I probably eat too much fast food.
B: You should try to eat more healthily. For example, you shouldn't eat fries for lunch. Perhaps you should eat a salad instead.

B. DISCUSS Think about the advice your partner gave you. Work in a group. Share the advice you received.

I eat too much fast food, so I should try to eat more healthily. For example, I ought to eat a salad for lunch instead of fries.

iQ PRACTICE Go online for more practice giving advice.
Practice ‣ Unit 2 ‣ Activity 14

UNIT ASSIGNMENT Conduct a class survey

OBJECTIVE ▶

In this assignment, you are going to interview three classmates about how their diets have changed. As you prepare your interview, think about the Unit Question, "Why do we change the foods we eat?" Use information from Listening 1, Listening 2, and your work in this unit to support your interview. Refer to the Self-Assessment checklist on page 50.

CONSIDER THE IDEAS

CATEGORIZE Work in a group. Each group member should fill out the following chart. Try to include at least three foods or dishes that represent a change in your diet—foods that you used to eat in the past but don't now or foods you eat now that you didn't before.

rice porridge

Food/Dish	Country of origin	Did you eat it in the past?	Do you eat it now?
rice porridge	not sure; eaten in my home country	Yes	No

In your group, quiz each other about your reasons.

A: I see you have started eating blueberries. Why?

B: They grow around here, and they taste good.

blueberries growing on a bush

PREPARE AND SPEAK

A. GATHER IDEAS Make a list of foods or dishes that you eat now but did not eat at some time in the past.

_____   _____

_____   _____

_____   _____

B. ORGANIZE IDEAS Choose one food or dish from your list in Activity A. Use the outline to help you prepare to talk about it. Do not write exactly what you are going to say. Just write notes to help you organize your ideas.

A NEW PART OF MY DIET

What's the name of the food or dish? _Kimchi_____

Where is it from? ___Korea_____

If it has ingredients, what are they? _vegetables, raddishes_
___carrots, garlic, ginger, chili pepper_____

How healthy is it? ___can eat everyday._____

Why have you added this food or dish to your diet? _____
___Natto, Udon, So Saladas,_____

_____

_____

TIP FOR SUCCESS

When making notes, don't write full sentences. Just write the important words.

C. SPEAK Complete these steps. Refer to the Self-Assessment checklist on page 50 before you begin.

1. Interview three students.

2. Ask them about the foods or dishes newly added to their diets from Activity B, and take notes in the chart below. When you talk about the food or dish that was newly added to your diet, use your notes from Activity B to help you. Do not read exactly what you wrote; just use your notes.

	Classmate 1	Classmate 2	Classmate 3
Food/Dish	Sushi	pumpkin soup	
Country	Japan	Hai-ti.	
Ingredients (if any)	rice, shrimp	pumpkin onion, garilc milk, water,	
Is it healthy?	It's healthy sea food is flesh.	vietmmm, A,C improve low cofories	
Why added to your diet?	delicious she likes rice and shrimp	delicious healthy, easy to cook	

3. When you finish, discuss your interviews in a group. Are there any foods that several people have added to their diets? Are there any especially common reasons for changing the foods that one eats?

iQ PRACTICE Go online for your alternate Unit Assignment.
Practice > Unit 2 > Activity 15

CHECK AND REFLECT

A. CHECK Think about the Unit Assignment as you complete the Self-Assessment checklist.

SELF-ASSESSMENT	Yes	No
I was able to speak easily about the topic.	☐	☐
My classmates understood me.	☐	☐
I used vocabulary from the unit.	☐	☐
I used quantifiers with count and noncount nouns.	☐	☐
I used links with /j/ and /w/.	☐	☐
I gave advice.	☐	☐
I predicted ideas about my partners' diets.	☐	☐

B. REFLECT Discuss these questions with a partner or group.

1. What is something new you learned in this unit?

2. Look back at the Unit Question—Why do we change the foods we eat? Is your answer different now than when you started this unit? If yes, how is it different? Why?

iQ PRACTICE Go to the online discussion board to discuss the questions.
Practice > Unit 2 > Activity 16

TRACK YOUR SUCCESS

iQ PRACTICE Go online to check the words and phrases you have learned in this unit. *Practice > Unit 2 > Activity 17*

Check (✓) the skills you learned. If you need more work on a skill, refer to the page(s) in parentheses.

CRITICAL THINKING	☐ I can predict topics or ideas. (p. 28)
LISTENING	☐ I can listen for causes and effects. (p. 33)
NOTE-TAKING	☐ I can take notes on causes and effects (p. 35)
VOCABULARY	☐ I can use adjective-noun collocations. (p. 41)
GRAMMAR	☐ I can use quantifiers with count and noncount nouns. (p. 43)
PRONUNCIATION	☐ I can link words with /j/ and /w/ sounds. (p. 45)
SPEAKING	☐ I can give advice. (p. 46)
OBJECTIVE ▶	☐ I can gather information and ideas to conduct a class survey on food preferences.

Psychology

3

In what ways is change good or bad?

A. Discuss these questions with your classmates.

1. What has been the biggest change in your life recently? How did it affect you?

2. Is there anything in your life right now that you would like to change?

3. Look at the photo. What kind of change is taking place? Would you ever make this kind of change in your life? How?

B. Listen to *The Q Classroom* online. Then answer these questions.

1. What changes have Marcus and Yuna made? How are they different?

2. What bad kinds of changes does Sophy mention?

3. What kinds of changes do Felix and Sophy talk about? Do you agree? Explain.

iQ PRACTICE   Go to the online discussion board to discuss the Unit Question with your classmates. *Practice > Unit 3 > Activity 1*

UNIT OBJECTIVE

Listen to a talk and an interview and gather information and ideas to participate in a group discussion about change.

As you listen to a speaker who mentions several events, take notes to help you remember them. You can set up a simple chart, noting key events in the left column and related details in the right. See Activity A below.

Listen for time expressions, such as years, months, ages, and phrases with words like *before*, *later*, *earlier*, and *finally*. For more practice with time expressions, see the Listening Skill on page 59.

The speaker might not mention events in correct time order. That's not a problem. Just note the information as you hear it. Later, review your notes and figure out the correct time order. Add small numbers to your notes to indicate which event came first, second, and so on. Then create a timeline to summarize the correct order of events. Label it with dates and key events.

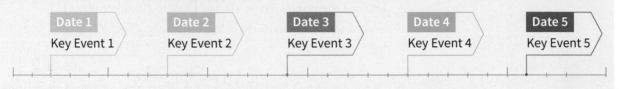

A. APPLY Here are some notes from a talk. The speaker did not give the events in time order. Read the notes and number the key events from 1 (the earliest) to 5 (the latest).

Key Event	Details
___4 US Civil War starts	April 1861; attack on Fort Sumter, South Carolina
___5 Lincoln elected president	Beat S. Douglas. 1860—just before Civil War
___2 Lincoln's 1st failure in US Senate race	1855; not direct election—Illinois legislature chose, not the public
___1 Lincoln drops out of politics for a while	1849-1854; disappointed by political fighting; wanted privacy
___3 Lincoln's 2nd failure in US Senate race	lost to S. Douglas; 1859

B. IDENTIFY Compare your answers with a partner. Discuss what information from the notes you used to determine your answers.

C. CREATE Use the information from Activity A to create a timeline like the one modeled in the Note-taking Skill box.

iQ PRACTICE Go online for more practice taking notes about events.
Practice ⟩ Unit 3 ⟩ Activity 2

LISTENING 1 — Shaped by Change, Promoting Change

OBJECTIVE ▶

You are going to listen to a talk about the Canadian philanthropist Jeffrey Skoll. He had to respond to unexpected changes in his life. He also went on to lead a group dedicated to creating changes in society. As you listen to the talk, gather information and ideas about the ways in which changes can be good and bad.

Jeffrey Skoll

PREVIEW THE LISTENING

A. PREVIEW What kinds of changes do you think Jeffrey Skoll might work to create? Check (✓) your predictions.

☐ Changes that increase his wealth

☐ Changes that help poor people

☐ Changes that make Canada more powerful

☐ Changes that improve health care

☐ Changes that help inform people about conditions around the world

☐ Changes that correct misunderstandings about history

☐ Changes that help put bad leaders in prison

B. VOCABULARY Read aloud these words from Listening 1. Check (✓) the ones you know. Use a dictionary to define any new or unknown words. Then discuss with a partner how the words will relate to Skoll's story.

as opposed to *(prep. phr.)*	**put together** *(v. phr.)*
eventually *(adv.)* 🔑	**quit** *(v.)* 🔑
found *(v.)* 🔑 OPAL	**resource** *(n.)* 🔑 OPAL
influence *(n.)* 🔑 OPAL	**turn upside down** *(v. phr.)*

🔑 Oxford 3000™ words   **OPAL** Oxford Phrasal Academic Lexicon

iQ PRACTICE Go online to listen and practice your pronunciation.
Practice > Unit 3 > Activity 3

WORK WITH THE LISTENING

A. LISTEN AND TAKE NOTES This chart contains some event-related notes from the talk about Skoll. As you listen, number the events in the order they occurred, and fill in the blanks.

iQ RESOURCES Go online to download extra vocabulary support.
Resources > Extra Vocabulary > Unit 3

Key Event	Details
_2_ father says he has cancer	Disturbing; Jeff ___14___ years old
_1_ Jeff read books with scary futures	On vacation before he was ___14___
Study:	
_3_ engineering U of _Turonto_	first degree
_5_ business school	later; got degree from _Stanford_
_4_ started computer-related businesses	before he went to _business_ school at Stanford
_6_ met Pierre O? (sp?)	to go full-time with Pierre running an _auction_ site
_7_ quit job _news-reporting company_	When?
_9_ became billionaire	after eBay stock went public
_8_ became president of eBay	year _2004_ ; Oscar-winning films
_11_ founded Participant Media	provides money for groups that try to solve _social and global problem_ ;
_10_ set up Skoll Foundation	founded in year _1999_

(handwritten margin notes:)
father
Influence book.
engineer experience
study in school
movie experience

B. CATEGORIZE Listen to the talk again. Check your notes from Activity A and revise them as necessary. Then number each event in your notes to show the time order, with "1" as the earliest.

C. IDENTIFY Read the questions. Circle the best answer for each question.

1. What was one good result of Jeff's father's illness?

   a. He grew up in Canada.

   b. Jeff learned a lesson.

   c. His family moved to California.

2. What was Jeff's reason for studying engineering and starting some businesses?

   a. He wanted to be a businessperson, not a writer.

   b. His family needed the money to pay medical bills.

   c. He planned to make enough money to afford to become a writer.

3. Jeff met Pierre at Stanford. In what way did this change their lives?

   a. Together they eventually had great success in their business.

   b. Together they helped create what we now call the Internet.

   c. Together they established the Skoll Foundation.

4. What event in eBay's history transformed Jeff and Pierre into billionaires?

   a. It changed its name to "eBay."

   b. The share price rose after the company went public.

   c. Sally Osberg became the company's president.

5. How does Participant Media relate to the idea of change?

   a. The company promotes positive changes to create social good.

   b. The company teaches tech people, financial people, and others to change.

   c. The company advises people on how to avoid harmful changes in life.

D. CATEGORIZE Read these statements. Write _T_ (true) or _F_ (false). Then correct each false statement to make it true.

_F_ 1. Jeff learned about possible scary futures by listening to stories his father told.

_T_ 2. Although writers don't make much money, Jeff still wanted to become a storyteller eventually.

_F_ 3. The speaker says that Jeff did not like suddenly having "all kinds of resources." _was a blessing_

_F_ 4. The Skoll Foundation closed in 2004 when Jeff founded Participant Productions. _is still in operation_

_T_ 5. Some of Participant Media's films have been very successful.

E. VOCABULARY Use the new vocabulary from Listening 1. Read the sentences. Then match each bold word with the correct definition below.

_c_ 1. The career counselor **put together** a talk about discovering what jobs might be good for you.

_d_ 2. This university, **as opposed to** most, has four 10-week terms each year, not semesters.

_a_ 3. The architect Frank Lloyd Wright had a strong **influence** on the designer of this house.

___ 4. The company's system was **turned upside down** when a new president took over.

___ 5. Harvard University is a very old institution, **founded** in 1636.

___ 6. If you save a little each month, **eventually** you will have enough money for a nice vacation.

___ 7. My grandfather **quit** his job at the factory to start his own bakery.

___ 8. Our state has enough **resources** to improve the road system, so we should.

ACADEMIC LANGUAGE

Complex prepositions are common in academic English. These are prepositions that are two or more words long. Listening 1 contains the complex preposition _as opposed to_, meaning _unlike_. It is used to indicate contrast, as in: _As opposed to most other birds, penguins cannot fly._ The prepositional phrase works as an adjective, modifying _penguins_.

_____| OPAL
Oxford Phrasal Academic Lexicon

a. _(n.)_ the power to affect, change, or control someone or something

b. _(v.)_ to leave your job, school, etc.

c. _(v. phr.)_ to build or make

d. _(prep. phr.)_ in contrast to

e. _(v. phr.)_ to make something very messy

f. _(adv.)_ in the end; after a long time

g. _(n.)_ a supply of something, a piece of equipment, etc., that is available for somebody to use

h. _(v.)_ to start an organization, institution, etc., especially by providing money

iQ PRACTICE Go online for more practice with the vocabulary.
Practice > Unit 3 > Activity 4

iQ PRACTICE Go online for additional listening and comprehension.
Practice > Unit 3 > Activity 5

 SAY WHAT YOU THINK

DISCUSS Discuss the questions in a group.

1. What did Jeff learn from his father's illness? How do you think learning that lesson affected his life?

2. How did Jeff react to becoming suddenly rich? Do you think you would react in the same way to sudden wealth?

3. One way Jeff is trying to promote social change is by making movies. Do you think movies can really have big social effects?

LISTENING SKILL Listening for time markers

When listening to a narrative, such as someone telling a story, it can be useful to listen for time markers. Time markers help to establish when something happened, for how long, etc. By listening for time markers, you can more easily understand past events and how they relate to one another. Here are some words and phrases that are commonly used as time markers:

now/nowadays	three days **ago**
before/after	**for** two weeks
then, next, after that	these days

A. IDENTIFY Listen again to the talk about Jeff Skoll. Draw a line to match each time marker (1–5) with an event (a–e).

1. One day when he was 14,

2. By the time he was 12 or 13,

3. In 1995,

4. Two years later,

5. Right after setting up the Skoll Foundation,

a. he and Pierre turned eBay into a public company.

b. his whole world turned upside down.

c. he hired Sally Osberg.

d. he had read authors like Orwell.

e. he graduated from business school.

B. CREATE Think about an important change that happened in your life. Make notes, using time markers to help clarify what happened and when.

C. DISCUSS Work with a partner. Discuss the important change in your life, using the notes you made in Activity B. Make sure you use time markers to help your partner understand.

iQ PRACTICE Go online for more practice listening for time markers.
Practice > Unit 3 > Activity 6

LISTENING 2 An Interview with Barbara Ehrenreich

OBJECTIVE ▶

You are going to listen to a radio interview with Barbara Ehrenreich, a well-known journalist and author. As you listen to the interview, gather information and ideas about how change is good and bad.

PREVIEW THE LISTENING

A. PREVIEW Why do you think a journalist might decide to "go undercover" to do research? Discuss your ideas with a partner.

B. VOCABULARY Read aloud these words from Listening 2. Check (✓) the ones you know. Use a dictionary to define any new or unknown words. Then discuss with a partner how the words will relate to the unit.

cope *(v.)*	research *(n.)* 🔑 OPAL
exhausted *(adj.)*	struggle *(v.)* 🔑
firsthand *(adv.)*	support (oneself) *(v.)* 🔑 OPAL
informed *(adj.)* OPAL	unemployed *(adj.)* 🔑
permanent *(adj.)* 🔑	wages *(n.)* 🔑

🔑 Oxford 3000™ words   **OPAL** Oxford Phrasal Academic Lexicon

iQ PRACTICE Go online to listen and practice your pronunciation.
Practice > Unit 3 > Activity 8

WORK WITH THE LISTENING

A. LISTEN AND TAKE NOTES Listen to the first part of the interview with Barbara Ehrenreich. As you listen, take notes on her reasons for going undercover.

iQ RESOURCES Go online to download extra vocabulary support.
Resources > Extra Vocabulary > Unit 3

Reasons for going undercover

need to experience something _____

a good way to _____

can write about experiences from a more _____

B. CATEGORIZE Read the statements. Listen to the second part of the interview. Write *T* (true) or *F* (false). Then correct each false statement to make it true.

___T___ 1. For *Nickel and Dimed*, Ehrenreich took several low-paying jobs.

___F___ 2. Ehrenreich found that it wasn't so difficult to cope financially.

___T___ 3. For *Bait and Switch*, Ehrenreich ~~researched~~ *was very* unemployment among white-collar workers.

___F___ 4. Ehrenreich found that life was more difficult for white-collar workers than unskilled workers. *Can be difficult for people at all*

___T___ 5. Ehrenreich is pleased that the changes she made were temporary. *levels*

___F___ 6. Ehrenreich didn't learn as much as she expected by going undercover. *learned more*

C. IDENTIFY Read the statements. Then listen again. Circle the answer that best completes each statement.

1. For her book *Nickel and Dimed*, Ehrenreich worked undercover in each job for _____.

   (a.) one month   b. three months   c. six months

2. While Ehrenreich was working undercover, she _____.

   a. studied hard   b. had a lot of fun   (c.) totally changed her life

3. Ehrenreich found that it was difficult to manage financially because _____ were so high.

   a. food prices   b. travel expenses   (c.) rents

4. Ehrenreich says that some of the jobs made her feel very _____.

   (a.) tired   (b.) bored   c. angry

5. Ehrenreich didn't expect *Nickel and Dimed* to be so _____.

   a. expensive   (b.) popular   c. easy to write

6. For her next book, *Bait and Switch*, Ehrenreich _____.

   (a.) used a false name   b. worked many jobs   c. did no research

7. For *Bait and Switch*, Ehrenreich pretended to be an unemployed _____ executive.

   a. human resources   b. account   (c.) public relations

8. Even though Ehrenreich claimed to have a lot of _____, she couldn't find any work.

   a. finances   (b.) experience   c. interests

Summarizing information you hear

When you **summarize** information that you hear, you give the main points but not all the details. You have to decide what information is important and what is not. Also, you find shorter ways to express information. This means that summaries are in your own words, not copied from the source.

College professors commonly require summaries—on tests or as part of homework assignments—as indications that you understood a listening passage. You can practice writing summaries on your own. After you have finished listening to any passage that is a minute or two long, write a summary of it for yourself. Then show your summary to a friend. Ask if your friend can understand what you heard just by reading or listening to the summary. If not, ask what other information your friend would want to know.

iQ PRACTICE Go online to watch the Critical Thinking Video and check your comprehension. *Practice > Unit 3 > Activity 7*

D. SYNTHESIZE Work with a partner. Listen again and take notes on what the speakers say about each book. Then write a summary of about 75 words about Barbara Ehrenreich's work. Your summary should mention both books.

E. DISCUSS Discuss the questions in a group.

1. Why do you think *Nickel and Dimed* was a best seller?

2. What qualities do you think a person needs to go undercover as Ehrenreich did? Would you like to try doing this? Why or why not?

**VOCABULARY
SKILL REVIEW**

In Unit 2, you learned about adjective-noun collocations. Can you find any adjective-noun collocations in Activity F? Underline them.

F. VOCABULARY Use the new vocabulary from Listening 2. Read the sentences. Circle the answer that best matches the meaning of each bold word or phrase.

1. It can be very difficult for people working in low-paying jobs to **cope**.

   a. manage financially   b. build relationships   c. be happy

2. After working for ten hours without a break, we were **exhausted**.

   a. very excited   b. very bored   c. very tired

3. It's hard to truly understand someone else's situation. Sometimes you need to experience it **firsthand**.

   a. quickly   b. directly   c. together

4. You need to know all the facts before you can make an **informed** decision.

   a. detailed   b. serious   c. educated

5. Agostino is always happy. He has a **permanent** smile on his face.

   a. constant   b. occasional   c. attractive

6. Sociologists are doing **research** on how people live in the poorest parts of the city.

   a. estimates   b. practice   c. studies

7. Many people who don't have jobs **struggle** when it is time to pay their bills.

   a. work hard   b. have difficulty   c. invest money

8. Many students at college don't receive money from their parents. They need to be able to **support themselves**.

   a. take care of themselves   b. live together   c. enjoy themselves

9. When the company closed down, many of its workers became **unemployed**.

   a. jobless   b. educated   c. sick

10. I enjoy my work, but the **wages** are too low for me to make a living.

    a. benefits   b. earnings   c. conditions

iQ PRACTICE   Go online for more practice with the vocabulary.
Practice › Unit 3 › Activity 9

WORK WITH THE VIDEO

A. PREVIEW Can a tough change like losing your job have good aspects? If so, what are they?

VIDEO VOCABULARY

Ivy League (*n.*) a group of eight universities in the United States with high academic standards, a high social status, and long-standing traditions

burned out (*adj.*) feeling as if you have done something too long and need a rest

head back (*v.*) return

ecstatic (*adj.*) very happy, excited, and enthusiastic

iQ RESOURCES Go online to watch the video about Christine Marchuska. *Resources > Video > Unit 3 > Unit Video*

B. SUMMARIZE Watch the video two or three times. Use the chart to summarize the positive and negative effects of the changes in Marchuska's life. Discuss them with a partner.

Positive effects	Negative effects

C. EXTEND Marchuska faced a difficult change in her life after she lost her job. However, she had some advantages that helped her overcome the job loss. With a partner, discuss what advantages she had. What would happen to someone who lost his or her job without each of those advantages?

SAY WHAT YOU THINK

SYNTHESIZE Think about the unit video, Listening 1, and Listening 2 as you discuss the questions.

TIP FOR SUCCESS

Be an active listener! Use expressions such as *Really?*, *Hmm, Yeah,* and *I see* to show that you are paying attention to the speaker.

1. Think about the changes that Jeff Skoll, Barbara Ehrenreich, and Christine Marchuska experienced. How were their experiences similar? How were they different?

2. What did each person learn from change? Who do you think learned the most? Explain your reasons.

VOCABULARY SKILL Using a word web

A **word web** is a diagram that connects words. You can use a word web to show the different meanings of a word.

- Start with a word with multiple meanings, such as *get*. Write the word in the middle circle of the word web.

- Next, look up the word in the dictionary. Some dictionaries have shortcuts, words that help you find the different meanings more quickly.

- Write each shortcut word in a circle surrounding the middle circle.

- Include an example sentence to help you understand the word and show how it is used in English.

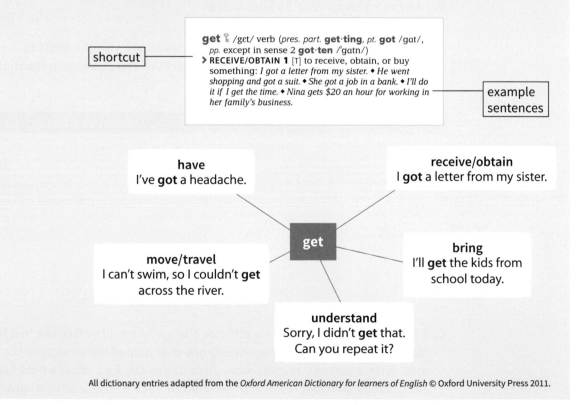

All dictionary entries adapted from the *Oxford American Dictionary for learners of English* © Oxford University Press 2011.

A. IDENTIFY Read the sentences. Then write the number of each sentence next to the correct shortcut in the word web. Use a dictionary to help you if necessary.

1. This town has changed a lot in recent years.

2. You need to change the light bulb in the kitchen.

3. It's quicker by bus, but you have to change twice.

4. Do you want to change before we go out?

5. Can you change a twenty-dollar bill?

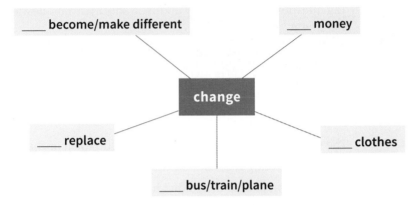

_____ become/make different   _____ money

change

_____ replace   _____ clothes

_____ bus/train/plane

B. INVESTIGATE Work with a partner. Use a dictionary to help you complete this word web with the verb _make_. Follow the steps in the Vocabulary Skill box.

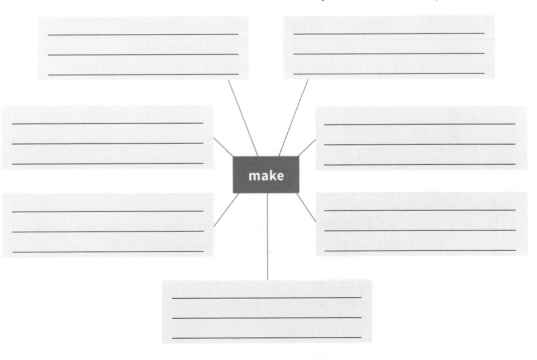

make

iQ PRACTICE Go online for more practice with using a word web.
Practice > Unit 3 > Activity 10

SPEAKING

OBJECTIVE ▶ At the end of this unit, you will take part in a group discussion about the advantages and disadvantages of change. Make sure to give reasons for your opinions and ask others for their reasons.

GRAMMAR Tag questions

Tag questions are common in everyday conversation. You can use a tag question to keep a conversation going by asking a person for her opinion about a situation.

Tag questions are formed by adding a short *yes/no* question at the end of a statement.

If the statement is positive, the tag question is negative.

⌐ Starting a new job **is** exciting, **isn't it**?

If the statement is negative, the tag question is positive.

⌐ They **aren't** moving home, **are they**?

The subject of a tag question is the pronoun form of the subject of the statement.

⌐ **You**'re starting your own business, aren't **you**?
⌐ **John** went to Australia, didn't **he**?
⌐ **Your friends** all have jobs, don't **they**?

The verb in a tag question is a form or part of the main verb in the statement.

If the statement contains an auxiliary verb or modal, use the auxiliary verb or modal in the tag question.

⌐ They**'re** curious about the world, **aren't** they?
⌐ All low-paid workers **should** get a raise, **shouldn't** they?
⌐ You **haven't** told anyone you're leaving, **have** you?

If the statement does not contain an auxiliary verb or modal, use a form of *do* in the tag question.

⌐ Your boss **trusts** you, **doesn't** he?
⌐ The crisis **got** better, **didn't** it?

iQ RESOURCES Go online to watch the Grammar Skill Video.
Resources > Video > Unit 3 > Grammar Skill Video

A. APPLY Use tag questions to complete the conversations. Then practice the conversations with a partner.

1. A: You're a journalist, _____?

    B: Yes, I am.

2. A: Simon never works on the weekend, _____?

   B: No, he doesn't.

3. A: They got married, _____?

   B: No, they didn't.

4. A: It's important to have good friends, _____?

   B: Yes, it is.

5. A: Susan should see her family more often, _____?

   B: Yes, she should.

6. A: Abed and Gary don't have permanent jobs, _____?

   B: No, they don't.

7. A: Valerie came here from France, _____?

   B: Yes, she did.

8. A: We can't afford an overseas vacation this year, _____?

   B: Yes, we can!

B. EXTEND Complete the sentences. Use tag questions. Then add three more sentences with tag questions of your own.

1. You don't like to get your hair cut, _____?

2. You haven't bought a new cell phone, _____?

3. You're not thinking of moving abroad, _____?

4. _____?

5. _____?

6. _____?

C. APPLY Work with a partner. Take turns asking and answering the questions from Activity B.

iQ PRACTICE   Go online for more practice with tag questions.
Practice > Unit 3 > Activity 11

iQ PRACTICE   Go online for the Grammar Expansion: additions with conjunctions. *Practice > Unit 3 > Activity 12*

PRONUNCIATION Intonation in tag questions

The **intonation** you use in tag questions is very important. Use falling intonation on the tag question when you think you know the answer and you are asking for confirmation. Use rising intonation on the tag question when you are not certain of the answer.

Asking for confirmation

Carol's never worked abroad, has she?   You can scuba dive, can't you?

Uncertain of the answer

Carol's never worked abroad, has she?   You can scuba dive, can't you?

A. IDENTIFY Listen to the sentences. Does the intonation rise or fall on each tag question? Check (✓) your answers.

	Rise	Fall
1. You've never been to Europe, have you?	☑	☐
2. Julie and Frank just had a baby, didn't they?	☐	☑
3. You're not looking for a new job, are you?	☑	☐
4. James is retiring next year, isn't he?	☐	☑
5. Kieron moved to New York last year, didn't he?	☑	☐
6. The new housing project was approved, wasn't it?	☐	☑

B. CLASSIFY Listen to the sentences. Does the speaker know the answer or not? Check (✓) your answers.

	Knows the answer	Doesn't know the answer
1. You've tried horseback riding, haven't you? ↷	☐	☑
2. Adapting to a new job can be hard, can't it? ↝	☑	☑
3. You wouldn't like to live in New York, would you? ↝	☑	☐
4. You're not afraid of change, are you? ↗	☐	☑
5. Travel is exciting, isn't it? ↝	☑	☐
6. You don't want to work for yourself, do you? ↘	☑	☐

C. IDENTIFY Listen again to the sentences from Activities A and B. Repeat the sentences. Use the same intonation that you hear.

D. IDENTIFY Work with a partner. Take turns reading the sentences from Activities A and B. Your partner will listen carefully and decide whether your intonation rises or falls.

iQ PRACTICE Go online for more practice with intonation in tag questions.
Practice > Unit 3 > Activity 13

SPEAKING SKILL Asking for and giving reasons

To better understand someone's point of view, you can ask the person to explain the **reasons** for his or her opinion. You can also help people understand your point of view by explaining your own reasons. Here are some phrases you can use to ask for or give reasons.

Asking for reasons	**Giving reasons**
Why do you think/say that?	because . . .
What are your reasons for saying that?	because of/due to . . .
Can you explain why . . . ?	The reason . . . is (that) . . .
	That's why . . .

To give several reasons for your point of view, you can introduce each reason with a phrase like these.

First (of all),   Also/Second,   Another reason/thing is . . .   Finally,

Listen to how the phrases are used in this conversation.

A: You know, I really don't think fishing is for me.

B: Oh yeah? **Why do you say that?**

A: Well, **first of all**, it's boring! **Also**, it's expensive to buy all the equipment, and **another thing** I hate is the smell of fish!

A. APPLY Listen to a conversation between two friends. Complete the conversation with the phrases you hear. Then practice the conversation with a partner.

TIP FOR SUCCESS

A good way to keep a conversation going is to ask questions. Asking for more information often helps a conversation become more interesting, too.

Jez: I haven't seen you for ages. How was your vacation in Spain?

Tom: It was great! I tried lots of new things—horseback riding, scuba diving . . . I even went to a bullfight in Madrid.

Jez: What? You went to a bullfight? I'm surprised.

Tom: Really? _____Why do you say that_____?
1

Jez: _____Because Its cool_____ it's cruel, isn't it? Why would you
2
want to watch that?

Tom: Well, _____First of all_____, it's an important part of the culture,
3
you know? _____Another reason is_____ it's really popular. Lots of tourists
4
were there. It's _____also_____ good to experience something
5
different for a change . . . I think.

B. DISCUSS Work in a group. Look at the activities in the box. Discuss which activities you would like to try. Give reasons for your ideas.

bungee jumping	camping	whitewater rafting
gardening	surfing	rock climbing
other: _____		

A: I'd like to try whitewater rafting. That sounds amazing.

B: Really? Why do you say that? I think it sounds scary.

A: Well, first of all, I love water sports, and another reason is that it looks very exciting.

iQ PRACTICE Go online for more practice asking for and giving reasons.
Practice > Unit 3 > Activity 14

UNIT ASSIGNMENT Take part in a group discussion

OBJECTIVE ▶

In this assignment, you are going to take part in a group discussion about the advantages and disadvantages of change. As you prepare for the group discussion, think about the Unit Question, "In what ways is change good or bad?" Use information from Listening 1, Listening 2, the unit video, and your work in this unit to support your discussion. Refer to the Self-Assessment checklist on page 74.

CONSIDER THE IDEAS

CATEGORIZE Work in a group. Think about the following important events that can occur in people's lives. Each event represents a big change. Discuss how each event might be good, bad, or both. Use phrases from the Speaking Skill box on page 71 to practice giving and asking for reasons.

changing your job	studying abroad	starting at a new school/college
moving to a new city	passing an exam	

PREPARE AND SPEAK

A. GATHER IDEAS Think about the events you discussed with your group. Choose one of the events that you have experienced yourself. Then write answers to the questions.

Which event did you choose?

Did you experience the good and bad aspects of the event you discussed with your group? What were they?

What did you learn from this event?

B. ORGANIZE IDEAS Create an outline. Use ideas from your discussion and your notes from Activity A. Think about change in general as you answer the questions. Do not write exactly what you are going to say. Just write notes to help you organize your ideas.

In what ways is change good?

In what ways is change bad?

What can we learn from change?

TIP FOR SUCCESS

When listening to your classmates, take notes of the main points each person makes. You can use these notes later when you want to ask questions.

C. SPEAK Discuss your ideas in a group. Do not read exactly what you wrote. Just use your notes. Use phrases from the Speaking Skill box on page 71 to give and ask for reasons. Decide who in your group has a view of change similar to your own. Refer to the Self-Assessment checklist below before you begin.

iQ PRACTICE Go online for your alternate Unit Assignment.
Practice > Unit 3 > Activity 15

CHECK AND REFLECT

A. CHECK Think about the Unit Assignment as you complete the Self-Assessment checklist.

SELF-ASSESSMENT	Yes	No
I was able to speak easily about the topic.	☐	☐
My group understood me.	☐	☐
I used vocabulary from the unit.	☐	☐
I used tag questions.	☐	☐
I used intonation in tag questions.	☐	☐
I asked for reasons for someone's opinion and gave reasons for my own opinions.	☐	☐
I summarized information from listening passages.	☐	☐

B. REFLECT Discuss these questions with a partner or group.

1. What is something new you learned in this unit?

2. Look back at the Unit Question—In what ways is change good or bad? Is your answer different now than when you started this unit? If yes, how is it different? Why?

iQ PRACTICE Go to the online discussion board to discuss the questions.
Practice > Unit 3 > Activity 16

TRACK YOUR SUCCESS

iQ PRACTICE Go online to check the words and phrases you have learned in this unit. *Practice > Unit 3 > Activity 17*

Check (✓) the skills you learned. If you need more work on a skill, refer to the page(s) in parentheses.

NOTE-TAKING	☐ I can take notes to show the time order of events. (p. 54)
LISTENING	☐ I can listen for time markers. (p. 59)
CRITICAL THINKING	☐ I can summarize information that I hear. (p. 63)
VOCABULARY	☐ I can use word webs. (p. 66)
GRAMMAR	☐ I can use tag questions. (p. 68)
PRONUNCIATION	☐ I can use intonation in tag questions. (p. 70)
SPEAKING	☐ I can ask for and give reasons. (p. 71)

OBJECTIVE ▶ ☐ I can gather information and ideas to participate in a group discussion about change.

How does advertising affect our behavior?

A. Discuss these questions with your classmates.

1. When you watch television, do you usually watch the commercials? What television ads can you think of right now?

2. How often do you click on Internet ads? Do you buy things online? If so, what kinds of things?

3. Look at the photo. Do you think ads can impact people's behavior? How?

B. Listen to *The Q Classroom* online. Then answer these questions.

1. What do Yuna and Sophy say about advertising they have seen? Do you think the same about yourself?

[handwritten: No pay attention]
[handwritten: No bought because of ads]

2. How do Marcus and Felix say advertising might influence our choices without our even knowing it? Do you agree?

[handwritten: hear name → famous]

iQ PRACTICE Go to the online discussion board to discuss the Unit Question with your classmates. *Practice > Unit 4 > Activity 1*

[handwritten notes: → affect behavior / create images → mind cuz / → go store → seems familiar / buy it / name is feel famous / keep mind / seen / shoes → have heard of / famous → trust this shop / buy it / hear]

UNIT OBJECTIVE

Listen to a radio show and a class discussion. Then listen to a lecture. Gather information and ideas to state and support your opinions in a group discussion on advertising.

LISTENING 1 Targeting Children with Advertising

OBJECTIVE ▶

You are going to listen to a radio show about advertising and then listen to a class discussion about the show. As you listen, gather information and ideas about how advertising affects our behavior.

PREVIEW THE LISTENING

A. PREVIEW In what ways do advertisers attract children's attention? Write down one or two ideas. Then share your ideas with the class.

B. VOCABULARY Read aloud these words from Listening 1. Check (✓) the ones you know. Use a dictionary to define any new or unknown words. Then discuss with a partner how the words will relate to the unit.

character *(n.)* 🔑 OPAL	regulate *(v.)*
claim *(n.)* 🔑 OPAL	scenario *(n.)* OPAL
give in *(v. phr.)*	take into account *(v. phr.)*
introduce *(v.)* 🔑 OPAL	unconsciously *(adv.)*
merchandise *(n.)*	worldwide *(adj.)* 🔑

🔑 Oxford 3000™ words   OPAL Oxford Phrasal Academic Lexicon

iQ PRACTICE Go online to listen and practice your pronunciation.
Practice › Unit 4 › Activity 2

WORK WITH THE LISTENING

🔊 **A. LISTEN AND TAKE NOTES** Look at the chart. Then listen to the radio show. As you listen, take notes in the chart about each speaker's idea(s) and opinion(s).

Speaker	Idea(s)/Opinion(s)
1. Interviewer	
2. Ann Fanton	
3. James Burney	

B. IDENTIFY Now use your notes to match one or two ideas or opinions with each speaker. Write the letters next to the speakers' names in the chart above.

a. It does not seem harmful to use cartoon characters in ads.

b. Using cartoon characters in ads is like turning children's friends into salespeople.

c. Children under eight years old are unable to think critically about advertising.

d. Parents on their own cannot effectively protect kids from harmful ads.

e. Some ads tell children to put pressure on their parents to buy things.

f. Kids sometimes influence decisions to buy expensive things, like vacations.

g. One car company has run car ads based on things that children wrote.

C. IDENTIFY Listen to the class discussion. In the *Discussion* column of the chart, check (✓) each topic that is mentioned in the discussion.

	Discussion	Radio Show
1. Effects of advertising on kids	☑	☐
2. Whether using cartoon characters is like using sports stars	☐	☐
3. Whether kids influence family decisions about spending	☐	☐
4. Dora, Elmo, Teletubbies	☐	☑
5. Whether very young kids can critically evaluate ads	☐	☐
6. The ability of parents to regulate kids' exposure to ads	☐	☐
7. Pokémon	☑	☐
8. Car ads by Honda	☐	☐
9. Amount spent on Harry Potter products	☑	☑
10. The connection between ads targeted to children and unhealthy diets	☐	☐

D. IDENTIFY Listen to the radio show and the discussion again. In the *Radio Show* column of the chart, check (✓) any topics that are mentioned in the radio show. Then compare charts with a partner.

E. CATEGORIZE Read the statements. Write *T* (true) or *F* (false). Then correct each false statement to make it true.

_F_ 1. Advertisers use characters like Pokémon mostly to teach children good behavior.

_T_ 2. Advertisers use children to influence what families buy.

_F_ 3. Parents have the power to control the advertising their children see.

_F_ 4. The teacher in the discussion allows his children to influence his car-buying decisions.

_T_ 5. A student in the discussion says that the character Harry Potter is attractive to parents.

_F_ 6. Products with Harry Potter characters have earned about $20 billion in sales in the United States.

F. VOCABULARY Use the new vocabulary from Listening 1. Read the sentences. Circle the answer that best matches the meaning of each bold word or phrase.

1. My favorite cartoon show had a **character** named Sylvia. She was a tall tree who solved mysteries.

    a. human actor   b. imaginary creature   c. product advertiser

2. Investigators are evaluating the **claim** that a certain man is 124 years old.

    a. lie   b. fact   c. statement

3. For months, we asked for permission to practice soccer in the park. Finally, the city **gave in**.

    a. refused   b. listened   c. agreed

4. Imagine this **scenario**: You're shopping for toothpaste for your children. One brand is on sale. Another brand has a picture of your son's favorite cartoon character on it. Which do you buy?

    a. future situation   b. part of a movie   c. story

5. The Pokémon characters were **introduced** in Japan in 1996.

    a. given names   b. originally designed   c. first brought out

6. Beloved movie characters can be found on all sorts of **merchandise**, such as book bags, T-shirts, coloring books, bed sheets, and much more.

    a. advertising   b. products for sale   c. clothing

7. If the government doesn't **regulate** hunting and fishing, some species of animals will be gone forever.

    a. control   b. support   c. eliminate

8. To estimate how long the trip will take, you have to **take into account** the heavy traffic.

    a. avoid   b. get stuck in   c. think about

9. I hope I didn't bother you by tapping my foot. That's something I do **unconsciously** when I'm nervous.

    a. by mistake   b. to get attention   c. without thinking

10. The **worldwide** system of air travel is a lot safer than it was 20 years ago.

    a. well-known   b. international   c. recent

iQ PRACTICE Go online for more practice with the vocabulary.
Practice > Unit 4 > Activity 3

iQ PRACTICE Go online for additional listening and comprehension.
Practice > Unit 4 > Activity 4

SAY WHAT YOU THINK

DISCUSS Discuss the questions in a group.

1. When you were a child, did you have any favorite characters from TV or movies? If so, which ones?

2. In your home culture, is it common for child-oriented characters to be used in advertising? Explain.

3. Think of an ad you have seen or heard recently that targeted children. What product was it advertising? How effective do you think it would be in increasing the sales of the product?

LISTENING SKILL Identifying fact and opinion

When you listen, it is important to identify what is a **fact** and what is someone's **opinion**.

A fact is something that is always true and can be proved.

⌈ Paris is the capital of France.
⌊ Soccer matches last 90 minutes.

An opinion is something that cannot be proved. People might disagree about an opinion.

⌈ Paris is the most beautiful city in the world.
⌊ Soccer is a great game for young children.

A. EVALUATE Listen to these statements from Listening 1. Decide whether each statement is a fact or an opinion. Circle your answers.

1. fact / opinion   2. fact / opinion   3. fact / opinion

B. EVALUATE Listen to statements from ads describing various products. Decide whether each statement is a fact or an opinion. Circle your answers.

1. fact / opinion   4. fact / opinion

2. fact / opinion   5. fact / opinion

3. fact / opinion   6. fact / opinion

TIP FOR SUCCESS

The next time you listen to the radio, focus on the ads. Listen carefully and try to identify what is fact and what is opinion.

iQ PRACTICE Go online for more practice identifying fact and opinion.
Practice > Unit 4 > Activity 5

The Influence of Online Ads

OBJECTIVE ▶

You are going to listen to a lecture about an online advertising technique. As you listen, gather information and ideas about how advertising affects our behavior.

PREVIEW THE LISTENING

A. PREVIEW Think about types of advertising other than ads on TV or in newspapers and magazines. In what other ways can advertisers reach you? Make a list of your ideas and then compare lists with a partner.

B. VOCABULARY Read aloud these words from Listening 2. Check (✓) the ones you know. Use a dictionary to define any new or unknown words. Then discuss with a partner how the words will relate to the unit.

add up to *(v. phr.)*	infer *(v.)* OPAL
the bottom line *(n. phr.)*	personal *(adj.)* 🍋 OPAL
criticize *(v.)* 🍋 OPAL	taste *(n.)* 🍋
disappear *(v.)* 🍋	uncomfortable *(adj.)* 🍋
evidence *(n.)* 🍋 OPAL	willingness *(n.)*

🍋 Oxford 3000™ words   OPAL Oxford Phrasal Academic Lexicon

iQ PRACTICE Go online to listen and practice your pronunciation.
Practice ▶ Unit 4 ▶ Activity 6

WORK WITH THE LISTENING

A. LISTEN AND TAKE NOTES Listen to the lecture. Take notes using the topics below.

iQ RESOURCES Go online to download extra vocabulary support.
Resources > Extra Vocabulary > Unit 4

Characteristics of online advertising

reserch, evidence, annoying, negative attitude, make money, ads, 2017, 4.7 billion $, CM, 98%, ads, know my taste, search, targeted, popups, messages

Effects on people

make ppl angry, make ppl uncomfortable, creepy, affects way use facebook, disturbing, behavior, complex way

B. IDENTIFY Listen again. Circle the answer that best completes each sentence according to the lecture.

ads make CM possible

1. The lecturer mentions Facebook's revenue to make the point that _____.

    a. Facebook is rich

    b. Facebook knows a lot about people

    c. Facebook depends a lot on advertising

2. The lecturer says that targeted advertising in the Internet era is different because _____.

    a. advertisers know more about people

    b. ads are tied to information and entertainment

    c. the content of ads is based on people's tastes

3. The lecturer liked the era before 1997 because _____.

    a. ads were more interesting

    b. she had more privacy

    c. she could give her contact information to stores

4. The lecturer says that even though we may not like online ads, they are not going away because _____.

    a. they are effective at getting people to buy

    b. many are exciting and entertaining

    c. companies have nowhere else to advertise

5. The lecturer mentions that one negative effect of targeted online advertising on Internet users is that such ads can _____.

   a. cost more to make, so prices of goods rise

   b. seem creepy to some people

   c. be hard for people nearby to see

C. CATEGORIZE Read these statements. Write *T* (true) or *F* (false). Then correct each false statement to make it true.

____ 1. About half of the money Facebook makes comes from selling ads.

____ 2. The Internet has "rewritten the rules" by allowing advertisers to target customers better.

____ 3. Pop-up ads that take up your whole screen are becoming more and more common.

____ 4. An ad that is too personal is considered "creepy."

____ 5. Because online advertising is so new, researchers don't know anything about its effects.

D. EXPLAIN How is "targeted advertising" different from other types of advertising? Why is it especially effective?

E. EXTEND Think of the targeted ads that you or someone you know has received. What products or services were advertised? Make a list. Note how interesting each product or service really is to the receiver of the ad.

CRITICAL THINKING STRATEGY

Evaluating the truthfulness of claims

To **evaluate** the truthfulness of a claim is to judge how accurate a statement is. Is it totally true, totally false, or partly true and partly false? Some claims relate to facts. You can check reliable sources and then evaluate how well the claim matches what the sources say.

Other claims are not so clearly true or false. They may be based at least partly on someone's opinion. When you evaluate claims like that, you ask yourself questions like *Does it make sense? Is it likely? How well informed is the speaker? How honest is the speaker? Does the speaker have any reason to lie?*

iQ PRACTICE   Go online to watch the Critical Thinking Video and check your comprehension. *Practice › Unit 4 › Activity 7*

F. DISCUSS Work with a partner. Imagine that, in a discussion of the lecture in Listening 2, one of your other classmates claims the following:

"Before they send you targeted ads, advertisers learn about you by watching you all day long through the cameras on your phone and your computers."

With your partner, evaluate that claim by discussing each of the questions below. Summarize your answers in the chart.

Questions	Answers
Does it make sense?	
Is it likely?	
How well informed is the speaker?	
How honest is the speaker?	
Does the speaker have any reason to lie?	

VOCABULARY SKILL REVIEW

In Unit 3, you learned that many words have more than one meaning. Use your dictionary to find out which words have different meanings. Make notes and use word webs to help you learn words and their meanings.

G. VOCABULARY Use the new vocabulary from Listening 2. Complete each sentence with the correct word or phrase.

add up to *(v. phr.)*	evidence *(n.)*	taste *(n.)*
the bottom line *(n. phr.)*	infer *(v.)*	uncomfortable *(adj.)*
criticize *(v.)*	personal *(adj.)*	willingness *(n.)*
disappear *(v.)*		

1. I know you like jazz, but it really doesn't fit my _____ in music.

2. This area used to be covered with forests, but the trees _____ about 150 years ago when the city grew.

3. The politician claimed the election was unfair, but she had no _____ that anyone cheated.

4. I really appreciate your _____ to help organize the picnic. If you hadn't volunteered, I would be really stressed out.

5. The manager didn't make eye contact with me throughout the entire interview. It made me feel very _____.

6. We've talked about a lot of things, but let's concentrate on the basics. _____ is that if we don't sell more products, we'll have to fire some employees.

7. Both parents in the family have good jobs, and their salaries together _____ a good income.

8. Parents, teachers, and students in the community quickly _____ the Board of Education's decision to drop the schools' art and music programs.

9. The man didn't actually tell me he was going for a hike, but I _____ it from the way he was dressed.

10. For your safety, do not give any _____ details about yourself to strangers.

iQ PRACTICE Go online for more practice with the vocabulary.
Practice > Unit 4 > Activity 8

WORK WITH THE VIDEO

A. PREVIEW Have you ever bought something because of an advertisement you saw online? Where did you see the ad? What did you buy?

VIDEO VOCABULARY

broadcast (*v.*) to send out to a wide audience by TV or radio

interact (*v.*) to communicate with, especially as you work, play, or spend time with them

campaign (*n.*) a series of planned activities that are intended to achieve a particular goal

engage (*v.*) to become involved with and try to understand someone

iQ RESOURCES Go online to watch the video about Internet advertising.
Resources > *Video* > *Unit 4* > *Unit Video*

B. CATEGORIZE Watch the video two or three times. Take notes in the chart.

Way(s) Internet Advertising Is Better for **Advertisers** than Non-Internet Ads	Way(s) Internet Advertising Is Better for **Consumers** than Non-Internet Ads
agent job	*acces produce directly*
what are people saying about	*direct customer*
influence the world	*↳ much more influence*
~~*direct customers*~~ *review the internet*	
can be much more specific	
easily talking to audience	

C. EXTEND What are some disadvantages to Internet advertising? Consider disadvantages for advertisers and for consumers.

SAY WHAT YOU THINK

SYNTHESIZE Think about the unit video, Listening 1, and Listening 2 as you discuss the questions.

1. Consider a country that all the members of your group know well. In that country, does the government do a good enough job of protecting families from ads aimed at children? If not, what else should the government do?

2. Targeted advertising is good for advertisers, but it only works if advertisers learn a lot about you. Do you think advertisers take away too much of an individual's privacy? If so, what changes could protect people's privacy?

VOCABULARY SKILL Using context clues to identify meaning

When you hear a word or phrase you don't know, it is sometimes possible to determine the meaning from the **context**. Try to identify the part of speech, and think about the words that surround it. Use this information to help you figure out what the word means.

☐ This magazine has a **circulation** of 100,000 a month.

Circulation is a noun. You can tell it refers to the number of copies of the magazine sold per month.

☐ We advertise a lot in video games because teenagers are our main **target**.

Target is a noun. You can tell it refers to the type of people that the ad is aimed at.

☐ **Infomercials** can mislead people into thinking they are watching a TV program.

Infomercial is the subject of the sentence and therefore a noun. You can see that it includes parts of two words you know: ***information*** and ***commercial***. The sentence tells you that infomercials can be confused with TV programs. From this context, you can see that an infomercial is a long commercial advertising a product.

A. IDENTIFY Read the sentences. Underline the context clues that help you determine the meaning of each bold word. Compare your ideas with a partner.

1. That ad is <u>so big</u> and <u>colorful</u>. It's very **eye-catching**.

2. That radio station plays the same ads all day. It's **tedious** to hear them over and over.

3. Commercials in **prime time** are the most expensive because the largest number of people watch TV then.

4. We really need a more aggressive marketing strategy to **push** this product if we want it to sell more.

5. The ads praising that new book are everywhere, but you shouldn't believe the **hype**. I read the book, and it's terrible.

6. The slogan was so **catchy** that I couldn't stop thinking about it for days.

B. APPLY Write each word from Activity A next to the correct definition. Compare your answers with your partner.

1. _____: *(v.)* to make something especially noticeable or attractive, so people will buy it

2. _____: *(adj.)* interesting or attractive to look at

3. _____: *(phr.)* the most popular time to watch TV

4. _____: *(n.)* advertising that makes something seem better than it is

5. _____: *(adj.)* easy to remember

6. _____: *(adj.)* boring and lasting a long time

iQ PRACTICE Go online for more practice using context clues to identify meaning. *Practice ⟩ Unit 4 ⟩ Activity 9*

SPEAKING

OBJECTIVE ▶ At the end of this unit, you will take part in a group discussion about how advertising affects our behavior. Make sure to give and support your opinions when you participate in the discussion.

GRAMMAR Modals expressing attitude

Modal verbs are special *auxiliary verbs* that help to express the attitude of the speaker. They are followed by the base form of the verb.

Prohibition:	Ads **must not** mislead anyone.
	They **can't** say anything false.
Strong obligation:	Ads **have to** be truthful.
	They **must** tell the truth.
Recommendation:	You **should** protect your personal information online.
	You **shouldn't** buy things that you don't need.
	If you ask me, there **ought to** be fewer ads on television.
No obligation:	You **don't have to** watch ads if you don't want to.

Note: *Must* and *must not* are more common in writing than in conversation.

 A. IDENTIFY Listen to the conversation. Circle the modal verbs you hear. Then practice the conversation with a partner.

Yvonne: Oh, look at that ad. Those poor animals! How can they show them suffering like that? I think it's terrible!

Maureen: Really? I think it's quite effective. They're trying to get your attention, you know.

Yvonne: Well, they (<u>don't have to</u> / <u>can't</u>) do it that way! It's not necessary, and it's upsetting.
1

Maureen: You (<u>must not</u> / <u>don't have to</u>) look at it if you don't want to.
2

Yvonne: That's not the point. That kind of advertising makes me really angry. I'm sure there's a law that says they (<u>don't have to</u> / <u>can't</u>) use animals like that.
3

Maureen: Maybe you (<u>should</u> / <u>have to</u>) complain, then.
4

Yvonne: Yes, I think I will. They (<u>shouldn't</u> / <u>don't have to</u>) be allowed to do that!
5

B. DISCUSS Discuss these questions in a group. Use modals to express your attitude when possible.

1. What do you think about ads that might make people angry?

2. Are there any types of advertising that should not be allowed?

iQ PRACTICE Go online for more practice using modals to express attitude. *Practice > Unit 4 > Activity 10*

iQ PRACTICE Go online for the Grammar Expansion: *would like, would prefer,* and *would rather. Practice > Unit 4 > Activity 11*

PRONUNCIATION *Part 1* Intonation in questions

Intonation is different for **yes/no questions** than it is for **wh- questions** (questions that begin with *who, what, when, where, why, which,* or *how*). The intonation rises at the end of *yes/no* questions. It falls at the end of *wh-* questions.

Here are some examples from the discussion in Listening 1.

Yes/no questions

Do you think it's true?

Can you guess which characters were at the top of the list?

Wh- questions

What do you remember most strongly?

What's wrong with that?

A. IDENTIFY Listen to the questions. Does the intonation rise or fall at the end? Circle your answers.

1. Do you spend a lot of money on advertising?   rise / fall

2. What do you think of that ad?   rise / fall

3. Is that ad misleading?   rise / fall

4. Does it have a special offer?   rise / fall

5. Why is there so much hype these days?   rise / fall

B. APPLY Listen again. Repeat the questions. Use the same intonation that you hear.

Statements as questions

Sometimes a statement is spoken with rising intonation to make it a question. This often happens if the speaker is surprised by what he or she has just heard.

Listen to how the intonation changes these statements into questions.

Statements

Food ads are popular.

Ads help to bring the world together.

Questions

Food ads are popular?

Ads help to bring the world together?

C. IDENTIFY Listen to the sentences. Are they spoken as statements or questions? Circle the correct answer and complete each sentence with a period or question mark.

1. Food ads are popular _?_   statement / (question)

2. Ads help to bring the world together ____   statement / question

3. The peak period starts at midnight ____   statement / question

4. Some ads are really popular ____   statement / question

5. Humorous ads are more effective ____   statement / question

6. More people watch TV in the evening than the daytime ____   statement / question

D. IDENTIFY Listen again. Then practice with a partner. Take turns saying different sentences from Activity C. Decide whether your partner is saying each sentence as a statement or a question.

iQ PRACTICE   Go online for more practice with intonation in questions.
Practice > Unit 4 > Activity 12

It is often useful to support your opinion by giving reasons and examples. Here are some phrases you can use when you want to give your opinion.

Giving opinions

I (don't) think (that)   If you ask me,
In my opinion/view,   As far as I'm concerned,

Here are some phrases you can use to support your opinion.

Supporting opinions

because/as   For instance,
For example,   To give you an example,

In my opinion, there's too much advertising on TV these days. **To give you an example**, a program I watched last night had ads almost every ten minutes! **If you ask me**, they shouldn't show ads in the middle of programs on TV.

iQ RESOURCES Go online to watch the Speaking Skill Video.
Resources ▸ Video ▸ Unit 4 ▸ Speaking Skill Video

A. APPLY Listen to this conversation. Complete the conversation with the phrases that you hear. Then practice the conversation with a partner.

Hugo: Hey. Look at this ad. It's got six famous people in it!

Peter: So what? _____, they should spend less on these expensive ads and lower the price of their clothes.
1

Hugo: Hmm. But I like seeing famous people in ads

_____ it makes it kind of cool.
2

Peter: _____, there are better ways to advertise things. _____, they could have
3 4
some facts and statistics or something. You know, some information.

Hugo: But it's an ad, right? _____, an ad
5
should get people's attention, and using famous people does that.

Peter: Well, I guess it's eye-catching, but I'm not sure how effective it is.

B. EVALUATE Work with a partner. What do you think of ads that feature famous people? Are they effective? Discuss these questions. Use phrases from the Speaking Skill box on page 94 to give and support your opinions.

iQ PRACTICE Go online for more practice giving and supporting your opinions.
Practice ▸ Unit 4 ▸ Activity 13

When discussing a topic, it can be useful to use a mind map. This is especially beneficial if you need to take notes on several different opinions. Using a mind map allows you to organize opinions and link supporting details to each opinion in a way that is easy to refer to later.

To make a mind map, first write the topic in the center and draw a box or circle around it. Then note all the different opinions by drawing a separate line for each opinion outward from the box or circle. You can add any supporting facts and details next to or below each opinion, as shown in the mind map below.

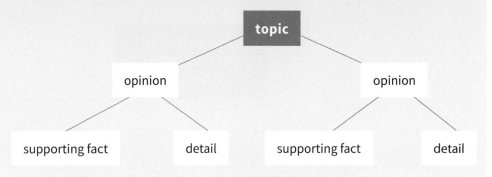

A. ANALYZE Study this mind map of a discussion on celebrity advertising. Notice how the opinions are noted separately along with their supporting ideas. Can you think of other ideas to add to the mind map?

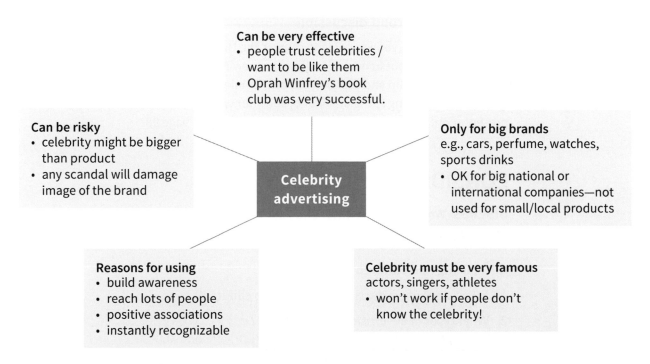

B. DISCUSS Discuss the topic of celebrity advertising using the mind map in Activity A to help you. Add any additional opinions and supporting details.

C. CREATE Fill in the mind map below to prepare for a discussion on what makes an advertisement effective. Write your opinions, supporting facts, and details in the empty boxes. Then discuss your opinions with a partner.

iQ PRACTICE Go online for more practice using a mind map to note opinions.
Practice > Unit 4 > Activity 14

UNIT ASSIGNMENT Take part in a group discussion

OBJECTIVE ▶

In this assignment, you are going to discuss the Unit Question, "How does advertising affect our behavior?" with a partner. Then you will summarize your discussion in a group and explain your own opinion. Use information from Listening 1, Listening 2, the unit video, and your work in this unit to support your presentation. Refer to the Self-Assessment checklist on page 98.

CONSIDER THE IDEAS

DISCUSS Work with a partner. Choose one of these topics and discuss your ideas. Use the questions to help you.

Advertising and children

1. What kinds of products are advertised to children?

2. What types of advertising are often used?

3. Should advertising to children be banned?

Online ads

1. How can advertisers keep online ads from being annoying?

2. What kinds of products or services can be most effectively advertised online?

3. Should the government limit the information that advertisers can collect about you from your online activity?

Status

1. What kinds of products are advertised as "high class"?

2. Who do you think is the target for these kinds of status ads?

3. Why are so many people influenced by this type of advertising?

Famous people in ads

1. Which famous people do you sometimes see in ads?

2. Why do advertisers use famous people in their ads?

3. Do you think celebrity endorsements are effective?

Advertising and you

1. Do you take more notice of ads on the web and social media than other forms of advertising?

2. What makes you remember an ad?

3. Are your purchasing decisions sometimes influenced by the ads you see?

PREPARE AND SPEAK

A. GATHER IDEAS Create a mind map. Write the topic you chose in the Consider the Ideas activity in the center. Then note your answers to each question (1–3) in the boxes around it. Add more information to help you note any additional ideas or opinions.

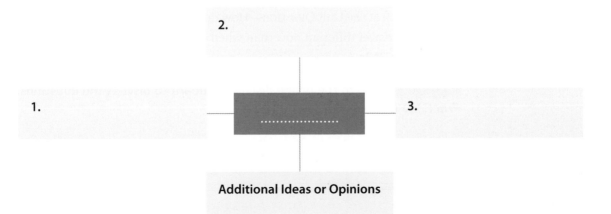

2.

1.

3.

....

Additional Ideas or Opinions

B. ORGANIZE IDEAS Support your opinions by adding facts and details. Make notes next to or below each opinion to explain your reasons.

C. SPEAK Have a group discussion about how advertisers can influence our behavior. Refer to the Self-Assessment checklist below before you begin.

1. Take turns presenting your ideas from Activity B.

2. You can refer to your notes, but do not read exactly what you wrote.

3. Give each student a turn as group leader.

iQ PRACTICE Go online for your alternate Unit Assignment.
Practice > Unit 4 > Activity 15

CHECK AND REFLECT

A. CHECK Think about the Unit Assignment as you complete the Self-Assessment checklist.

SELF-ASSESSMENT	Yes	No
I was able to speak easily about the topic.	☐	☐
My partner and group understood me.	☐	☐
I used vocabulary from the unit.	☐	☐
I used modals expressing attitude.	☐	☐
I used correct intonation in questions.	☐	☐
I gave and supported my opinion.	☐	☐
I helped my group evaluate advertising claims.	☐	☐

B. REFLECT Discuss these questions with a partner or group.

1. What is something new you learned in this unit?

2. Look back at the Unit Question—How does advertising affect our behavior? Is your answer different now than when you started this unit? If yes, how is it different? Why?

iQ PRACTICE Go to the online discussion board to discuss the questions.
Practice > Unit 4 > Activity 16

TRACK YOUR SUCCESS

iQ PRACTICE Go online to check the words and phrases you have learned in this unit. *Practice › Unit 4 › Activity 17*

Check (✓) the skills you learned. If you need more work on a skill, refer to the page(s) in parentheses.

LISTENING ☐ I can identify fact and opinion. (p. 82)

CRITICAL THINKING ☐ I can evaluate the truthfulness of a speaker's claims. (p. 85)

VOCABULARY ☐ I can use context clues to identify meaning. (p. 89)

GRAMMAR ☐ I can use modals to express attitude. (p. 91)

PRONUNCIATION ☐ I can use correct intonation in questions. (pp. 92 & 93)

SPEAKING ☐ I can give and support my opinions. (p. 94)

NOTE-TAKING ☐ I can use a mind map to note opinions. (p. 95)

OBJECTIVE ▶ ☐ I can gather information and ideas to state and support my opinions in a group discussion on advertising.

5 Behavioral Science

NOTE-TAKING	separating risks and outcomes using a chart
LISTENING	listening for different kinds of numbers
CRITICAL THINKING	evaluating the strength and relevance of evidence
VOCABULARY	word families
GRAMMAR	past perfect
PRONUNCIATION	contraction of *had*
SPEAKING	giving a short presentation

Does taking risks change our lives?

A. Discuss these questions with your classmates.

1. What are some risks that people take? Why do they take them?

2. Are some risks more dangerous than others? Do some provide greater rewards? In what ways?

3. Look at the photo. What kind of a risk is this person taking? Would you ever take this kind of risk? Why or why not?

B. Listen to *The Q Classroom* online. Then answer these questions.

1. What types of risks does Felix mention?

2. According to Marcus, what can be one result of taking social risks?

3. What kind of risks do Yuna and Sophy talk about? Do you agree with them? Why or why not?

iQ PRACTICE Go to the online discussion board to discuss the Unit Question with your classmates. *Practice > Unit 5 > Activity 1*

UNIT OBJECTIVE

Listen to a podcast and a report and gather information and ideas to give a short presentation on a risk you have taken.

When people take risks, they do so because they want one or more outcomes. An outcome is a result, or an effect, of taking a certain action. When listening to a speaker talking about risks and outcomes, you can list the risks and outcomes for an action separately in a chart.

Action: Moving to a new city	
Risks	Desired Outcomes
• far away from friends/family	• find a better job in field
• have to quit job	• take classes at the university
• no apartment	• meet new people

Signposts to listen for:

One possible risk is . . .	It threatens . . .
This is risky because . . .	She wants / hopes to . . .
One danger of this is . . .	We take the risk in order to . . .
You risk . . .	. . . far outweighs any risk.

A. IDENTIFY Listen to this excerpt from a presentation about a new hobby. Then answer the questions.

1. What action does the speaker talk about? _Try to Some thing_ ^(Caya)

2. What were some risks?

   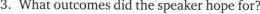 _Caya   lose   my_

   She can losen soccer,
   spot in

3. What outcomes did the speaker hope for?

   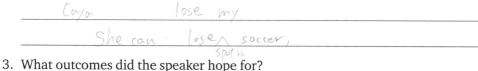 _I want Tv Try something new._

   Meeting new people,

B. RESTATE Listen again. With a partner, summarize the speaker's points in the chart below.

Action:

Risks	Outcomes

iQ PRACTICE Go online for more practice separating risks and outcomes using a chart. *Practice > Unit 5 > Activity 2*

LISTENING SKILL Listening for different kinds of numbers

Speakers often support their ideas with specific information including dates, ages, percentages, fractions, and amounts of money.

Listen for the numbers and for words that tell you what kind of data each number represents.

Listen to these examples.

In 2005	20 hours
On May 15	40 percent
Ages 13 through 19	Two thirds
Adults, aged 20 through 35	One quarter
10,000 people	$500 (dollars)
400 participants	€100 (euros)

Listen to this excerpt from a lecture and notice the numbers you hear.

In one study in Germany, researchers did an experiment with 105 people between the ages of 8 and 22 in which the people played a game and tried to win between 3 and 32 euros.

A. IDENTIFY Listen to and complete the sentences about activities.

1. We asked _____2,000 people_____ about their weekend activities.

2. Most people spent _____5 hours_____ a day watching TV.

3. Those _____aged 16 to and 24_____ spent the most time on social media.

4. Americans spent _____37 billion doll_____ on sports equipment in 2016.

5. Like other dangerous sports, snowboarding is becoming more popular, up _____51 %_____ since _____1919_____.

6. Mountain biking has _____8.6 million_____ participants.

7. _____3 8 %_____ of people who race mountain bikes have had injuries.

8. One in _____too 141,000_____ bicyclists die in bicycle accidents.

9. About _____15 one fifth_____ of Americans over the age of _____55_____ exercise on any given day.

10. Older people may take fewer risks because an important chemical in the brain decreases by _____ten per_____ every _____ten years._____.

B. APPLY With a partner, ask and answer questions about the number-related information in Activity A.

A: How many people did they ask about weekend activities?
B: Two thousand.

iQ PRACTICE Go online for more practice listening for different kinds of numbers. *Practice > Unit 5 > Activity 3*

LISTENING 1

OBJECTIVE ▶

A Lifetime of Risks

Podcast

You are going to listen to a podcast about risk-taking at different stages of life. As you listen to the podcast, gather information and ideas about how taking risks changes our lives.

PREVIEW THE LISTENING

A. PREVIEW Look at the list of risks that many people take. At what age do you think most people take them? Write the ages.

_____ starting a business

_____ taking first steps

_____ driving fast

_____ changing careers

_____ joining a new club

_____ finding new friends

_____ traveling to another country

_____ investing money

_____ trying a dangerous sport

_____ moving to another city/country

ACADEMIC LANGUAGE
The corpus shows
that *the development
of* is often used in
academic speaking.
*The development
of . . . is . . .*
*. . . leads to the
development of . . .*

_____ OPAL

Oxford Phrasal Academic Lexicon

B. VOCABULARY Read aloud these words from Listening 1. Check (✓) the ones you know. Use a dictionary to define any new or unknown words. Then discuss with a partner how the words will relate to the unit.

cycle *(n.)* ⚷ OPAL	financial *(adj.)* ⚷ OPAL
decline *(v.)* ⚷ OPAL	growth *(n.)* ⚷ OPAL
development *(n.)* ⚷ OPAL	judgment *(n.)* ⚷ OPAL
encourage *(v.)* ⚷ OPAL	survival *(n.)* OPAL
explore *(v.)* ⚷ OPAL	tendency *(n.)* OPAL

⚷ Oxford 3000™ words   **OPAL** Oxford Phrasal Academic Lexicon

iQ PRACTICE Go online to listen and practice your pronunciation.
Practice › Unit 5 › Activity 5

WORK WITH THE LISTENING

A. LISTEN AND TAKE NOTES Listen to the podcast. Complete the chart with examples of risky behavior at each life stage and outcomes of that behavior.

get fun

iQ RESOURCES Go online to download extra vocabulary support.
Resources › Extra Vocabulary › Unit 5

take risk - money (likely)

Life Stage	Risks	Outcomes
Children	1. ∘ *wat act without thinking* 2. ∘ *fall down* ∘ *run into the street after a ball*	1. *learn to walk* 2. *get the ball*
Teenagers	1. *challenge other play sport* 2. 3. *sport, meet people* *con driving fast*	1. *develop skill* *make new friends* 2. *survival - driving fast* 3. *holmon development*
Young adults	1. *re ceeational risks* 2. *skydiving - banger*	1. *fun*
Older adults in some countries	1. move to . . . *New city* *New opportuni'y*	1. *better life*

B. APPLY Look at your notes. Discuss them with a partner and make any necessary changes. Think about people you know at different stages of life. What kinds of risks do they take?

C. EXTEND Listen to the excerpt. Complete the notes with details about the research studies. Notice the numbers you hear.

Study 1	**Where:** Germany
	# Participants: _20,000_
	Age range: not given, includes older people
	Findings: Older people less likely to take risks with _money_.
main outcome	_Men_ take more than _woman_. _Tall pap_ take more than _short ones_.

Study 2	**Where:** not given
	# Participants: ~~5002~~ _52P_
	Age range: _F015~ #8-93_
	Findings: Overall, risk-taking _decreases_ as we get older. Men less likely to take _many_ risks. Women less likely to take _financial_ risks. _Social_ risks decline after young adulthood. _Recreational_

Study 3	**Where:** _77_ countries, including Germany, _the US_, Russia, Pakistan, Mali, and _Naijelia._ _Nigeria._
	# Participants: Almost 150,000
	Age range: _15-99_
	Findings: In some countries, men and women take _more_ risks throughout their _lifetimes_ because life is _difficult_.

CRITICAL THINKING STRATEGY

Evaluate the strength and relevance of evidence

When we **evaluate** evidence, we frequently look at two things: strength and relevance. Evidence is **strong** if it includes specific facts such as numbers, dates, and sources of information. This kind of evidence can be checked.

| *Researchers at Lincoln University found . . .* | We know the source. |
| *Eighty percent of the reef has died.* | We can check specific numbers. |

Evidence that is vague and general is considered **weaker**.

| *Some people say . . .* | We don't know the source. |
| *Most people think . . .* | There isn't a specific fact to check. |

Evidence is **relevant** if it is directly related to the claim and proves the point.

> *Twenty-one percent of accidents involving teenaged drivers involved speeding.*

This makes a connection with the claim.

Evidence is **not relevant** if it introduces a new topic or is a side comment.

> *Teenagers listen to loud music when they drive.*

This is a side comment not directly connected to the claim.

iQ PRACTICE Go online to watch the Critical Thinking Video and check your comprehension. *Practice > Unit 5 > Activity 4*

D. EVALUATE Read the excerpts. Rate each piece of evidence in terms of strength and relevance (1 lowest, 5 highest). Then compare with a partner.

1. **Claim:** Taking risks at this time prepares us to face challenges as adults.

   Evidence: Positive risk-taking like playing a sport or meeting new people has clear benefits because we develop skills and friendships.

   Evaluation: Strength 1 2 3 4 ⑤   Relevance 1 2 3 4 ⑤

2. **Claim:** Teenaged brains are more sensitive to interactions with peers or other teenagers.

   Evidence: When friends exclude us, our brains have a strong negative reaction.

   Evaluation: Strength 1 2 ③ 4 5   Relevance 1 2 3 ④ 5

3. **Claim:** Poor teenagers! It's an endless cycle.

   Evidence: Like when I exercise to lose weight but then need to eat more.

   Evaluation: Strength ① 2 3 4 5   Relevance ① 2 3 4 ⑤

4. **Claim:** Researchers have long thought that risk-taking declines with age, especially taking financial risks.

   Evidence: One study at the University of Bonn of 20,000 people found that older people are much less likely to take risks with their money.

   Evaluation: Strength 1 2 3 4 ⑤   Relevance 1 2 3 4 ⑤

5. **Claim:** Researchers have long thought that risk-taking declines with age, especially taking financial risks.

   Evidence: They looked at information from 77 countries, a total of almost 150,000 people aged 15 to 99, 52 percent of whom were women.

   Evaluation: Strength 1 2 3 4 5   Relevance 1 2 3 4 5

E. CATEGORIZE Read the statements. Listen to the podcast again. Write *T* (true) or *F* (false). Write supporting information from the listening. Then correct each false statement to make it true.

_F_ 1. Teenagers, like younger children, take impulsive risks.

Supporting information: _As children become adolescents, they . . ._

_T_ 2. One reason teenagers take risks is to help them prepare for adulthood.

Supporting information: _____

_F_ 3. Teenagers are generally good at making judgments about dangerous situations.

Supporting information: _____

_T_ 4. Taking risks can help our brains develop.

Supporting information: _____

_F_ 5. Men and women have a tendency to take the same kinds of risks throughout their lifetimes.

Supporting information: _____

_T_ 6. Living in a place that has a lot of problems makes it more likely you will take risks.

Supporting information: _____

F. EVALUATE With a partner, evaluate the supporting information in Activity E in terms of its strength and relevance.

G. VOCABULARY Use the new vocabulary from Listening 1. Complete each sentence with the correct word.

cycle *(n.)*	encourage *(v.)*	growth *(n.)*	tendency *(n.)*
decline *(v.)*	explore *(v.)*	judgment *(n.)*	
development *(n.)*	financial *(adj.)*	survival *(n.)*	

1. Our ability to show good __judgment__ gets better with age. We make better decisions.

2. Parents should __encourage__ their children to take certain risks, such as participating in sports or trying a new activity.

3. As a child psychologist, she is very interested in the __development__ of decision-making skills in young children.

4. Often people without a lot of money are afraid to take __financial__ risks.

5. You've gotten so tall. I didn't realize so much __growth__ was possible in a year.

6. She was lost at sea in terrible conditions with little food for months. Her __survival__ depended on a lot of skill and a little luck.

7. I enjoy the _____cycle_____ of seasons every year—spring, summer, fall, winter and then back around again.

8. For many people, their ability to remember _____declines_____ with age.

9. I believe that humans have a need to _____explore_____ their world. That's why babies learn to walk and why adults travel to new places.

10. Most teenagers have a _____tendency_____ to want to spend more time with their friends than with their families.

iQ PRACTICE   Go online for more practice with the vocabulary.
Practice > Unit 5 > Activity 6

iQ PRACTICE   Go online for additional listening and comprehension.
Practice > Unit 5 > Activity 7

SAY WHAT YOU THINK

DISCUSS Discuss the questions in a group.

1. Were you surprised about the risks people take at different times in their lives? Why or why not?

2. Think of other risks people usually take at different stages of their lives. Then share them with the class.

3. Name some risks you or people you know have taken. What outcomes did you or they hope for? Did you or they get those outcomes?

LISTENING 2   Science on the Edge

OBJECTIVE ▶

You are going to listen to a report on scientists with risky jobs. As you listen to the report, gather information and ideas about how taking risks changes our lives.

PREVIEW THE LISTENING

A. PREVIEW Which fields of science do you think are risky?

☐ drug research

☐ laboratory research

☐ meteorology (weather)

☐ studying volcanoes

☐ underwater exploration

☐ your idea: _____

B. VOCABULARY Read aloud these words from Listening 2. Check (✓) the ones you know. Use a dictionary to define any new or unknown words. Then discuss with a partner how the words will relate to the unit.

discover *(v.)* ⚷ OPAL	previous *(adj.)* ⚷ OPAL
invention *(n.)* ⚷	prove *(v.)* ⚷
investigate *(v.)* ⚷ OPAL	reputation *(n.)* ⚷
locate *(v.)* ⚷ OPAL	retire *(v.)* ⚷
mystery *(n.)* ⚷	solve *(v.)* ⚷ OPAL

⚷ Oxford 3000™ words   **OPAL** Oxford Phrasal Academic Lexicon

iQ PRACTICE Go online to listen and practice your pronunciation.
Practice > Unit 5 > Activity 8

WORK WITH THE LISTENING

A. LISTEN AND TAKE NOTES Listen to the report. Take notes in the chart as you listen.

iQ PRACTICE Go online to download extra vocabulary support.
Resources > Extra Vocabulary > Unit 5   However, he likes jobs Because,

	Risks taken	Outcomes
Paul Flaherty		
Tina Neal		

B. EXPLAIN Work with a partner. Answer the questions with information from the chart.

1. What risks do they both take?

2. What outcomes do both hope for?

C. CATEGORIZE Read the statements. Write *T* (true) or *F* (false). Then correct each false statement to make it true.

_F_ 1. Flaherty and Neal work in the same scientific field.

_T_ 2. Weather is one of the biggest risks they face.

_T_ 3. Both scientists gather information that can be used to help predict natural disasters.

_F_ 4. Unfortunately, there isn't much they can do to control or lower their risks.

D. IDENTIFY Listen again. Who is the detail about? Write *F* (Flaherty), *N* (Neal), or *B* (both) for each description.

_F_ 1. is a pilot

_B/N_ 2. flies a lot as part of the job

___ 3. makes maps of safe areas

_F_ 4. provided information on Hurricane Katrina

_N_ 5. lives in Alaska

_B_ 6. uses data to protect people

_F_ 7. works for the National Oceanic and Atmospheric Administration

_B/N_ 8. works for the US Geological Survey

E. ANALYZE Complete the Venn diagram with information about the two scientists.

Paul Flaherty   Both   Tina Neal

F. DISCUSS Discuss the questions in a group.

1. Why do you think Flaherty and Neal are willing to take risks? Do you think they are different from most people? If so, how?

2. What other weather problems or natural disasters do we need to learn more about? What risks are involved in investigating them?

VOCABULARY SKILL REVIEW

In Unit 4, you learned how to use context clues to identify meaning. In Activity G, underline the clues in the sentences that help you identify the meaning of the bold words.

G. VOCABULARY Use the new vocabulary from Listening 2. Read the sentences. Then write each bold word next to the correct definition.

1. Marie Curie was the first person to **discover** the elements polonium and radium.

2. My uncle's **invention** is a new machine that makes coffee and a doughnut at the same time.

3. For your next paper, I want you to **investigate** a topic that is interesting to you.

4. The police were unable to **locate** the stolen artifact.

5. Until recently, the nature of the planet Mars has been a **mystery**.

6. On my **previous** trip to Italy, I went to Venice, but I'm not going there this time.

7. Columbus was able to **prove** the earth was round.

8. That university has a very good **reputation**.

9. Dr. Arnesen enjoys his job so much, he says he never wants to **retire**.

10. Some of life's problems are too difficult for people to **solve** on their own.

a. _____locate_____ (v.) to find the exact position of someone or something

b. _solve_ _investigate_ (v.) to find a way of dealing with a problem or situation

c. _____previous_____ (adj.) coming or happening before or earlier

d. _____investigate_____ (v.) to try to find out all the facts about something

e. _____invention_____ (n.) something that is made for the first time

f. _____retire_____ (v.) to stop working, usually because you have reached a certain age

g. _____reputation_____ (n.) the opinion that people in general have about someone or something

h. _____prove_____ (v.) to use facts or evidence to show something is true

i. _____mystery_____ (n.) a thing that you cannot understand or explain

j. _____discover_____ (v.) to find or learn something that no one knew or had found before

iQ PRACTICE Go online for more practice with the vocabulary.
Practice > Unit 5 > Activity 9

WORK WITH THE VIDEO

A. PREVIEW Do you like to explore new places? Why? Why not?

VIDEO VOCABULARY

expedition (*n.*) a long trip for a special purpose

rival (*n.*) a person, group, or thing that is competing with another

eastward (*adv.*) toward the east

strait (*n.*) a narrow area of water that joins two larger seas or oceans

capture (*v.*) to take someone prisoner

voyage (*n.*) a long trip by ship or in space

circumnavigation (*n.*) the act of sailing around something, especially all the way around the world

iQ RESOURCES   Go online to watch the video about Magellan's voyage.
Resources > Video > Unit 5 > Unit Video

B. CATEGORIZE Watch the video two or three times. Take notes in the first part of the chart.

Risks	Outcomes
Notes from the video:	
My ideas:	

C. EXTEND What are the risks or outcomes of other voyages or expeditions that you know about? Write your ideas in the chart above.

SAY WHAT YOU THINK

SYNTHESIZE Think about Listening 1, Listening 2, and the unit video as you discuss the questions.

1. What kind of risks do people take that are primarily for personal benefit? What risks do people take for the benefit of others?

2. Are you a person who often takes risks? Why or why not? Do you think that will change?

3. How have the risks taken in the unit changed the world? What does this say about taking risks?

VOCABULARY SKILL Word families

One way to increase your vocabulary is to understand **word families**. Word families consist of words that come from the same root and are related in form. They usually include several different parts of speech. For example, a noun may have an adjective and a verb form. The ending of the word often indicates the part of speech.

> **in·vent** 🔊 Ⓢ /ɪnˈvɛnt/ *verb* [T] **1** to think of or make something for the first time: *Who invented the sewing machine?* ◆ *When was the camera invented?* **2** to say or describe something that is not true: *I realized that he had invented the whole story.* ▶ **in·ven·tor** /-ər/ *noun* [C]
>
> **in·ven·tion** 🔊 /ɪnˈvɛnʃn/ *noun* **1** [C] a thing that has been made or designed by someone for the first time: *The microwave oven is a very useful invention.* **2** [U] the action or process of making or designing something for the first time: *Books had to be written by hand before the invention of printing.* **3** [C, U] telling a story or giving an excuse that is not true: *This story is apparently a complete invention.*
>
> **in·ven·tive** /ɪnˈvɛntɪv/ *adj.* having new and interesting ideas ▶ **in·ven·tive·ness** *noun* [U]

When you look up new words in the dictionary, look at the other words in the same word family. By doing this, you can add several new words to your vocabulary.

Another benefit of understanding word families is that when you see new words that look similar to words you already know, you can use your knowledge to figure out their meaning.

All dictionary entries adapted from the *Oxford American Dictionary for learners of English* © Oxford University Press 2011.

A. CATEGORIZE Work with a partner. Complete the word family chart with any forms of the words you know. Use a dictionary to check your answers.

Verb	Noun	Adjective	Adverb
invent	inventor	inventive	inventively
develop	developer	developmental	developmentlly
discover	discovery		
explore	exploration	exploratory	
~~financial~~ finance	financial	financial	financially
locate	location		
prove	proof	proven	
solve	solution		

financie

B. APPLY Complete each sentence with an appropriate word from your completed chart in Activity A.

1. A _developmental_ psychologist is interested in how children grow and change.

2. I can't _solve_ this math problem.

3. The scientist made an important new _discovery_.

4. Independent TV producers _solve_ their programs in different ways, from credit cards to private investors to personal savings.

5. The _solution_ to the problem is at the back of the book.

6. Having too much credit card debt can lead to _develop financial_ disaster.

7. Scientists have never found real _proof_ ~~discovery~~ that aliens exist.

8. We decided not to buy the house because of its _location_. It was too close to the freeway.

9. I can't _prove_ he took my money, but I think he did.

10. Outer space and the deep ocean are the last great regions for human _exploration_ ~~location~~. They are difficult for people to live in, so we don't know much about them.

iQ PRACTICE Go online for more practice with word families.
Practice > Unit 5 > Activity 10

SPEAKING

OBJECTIVE ▶

At the end of this unit, you will give a short presentation on a risk you have taken. Make sure to clearly explain your reasons for taking that risk.

GRAMMAR Past perfect

Use the **past perfect** to show the relationship between two events or actions that happened in the past. Use the past perfect to describe the first event or action that happened. Use the **simple past** to describe the second event or action.

Past perfect *(1st event)*	**Simple past** *(2nd event)*
I **had driven** for five hours.	I **went** straight to bed without dinner.
The match **had** already **started**.	We **arrived** late.

Use the past perfect with past time clauses that begin with *when*, *before*, *by the time*, and *until*.

Past perfect *(1st event)*	**Simple past** *(2nd event)*
He **had been** at work for hours	<u>when</u> we **called** him.
Paul **had driven** for an hour	<u>before</u> he **noticed** he had a flat tire.
They **had** already **eaten** dinner	<u>by the time</u> I **got** home.
I **hadn't heard** anything about it	<u>until</u> I **read** the paper this morning.

Note: The past perfect is often used with the adverbs *already, yet, never, ever,* and *just*.

iQ RESOURCES Go online to watch the Grammar Skill Video.
Resources > Video > Unit 5 > Grammar Skill Video

A. COMPOSE Read the pairs of sentences. Write 1 next to the sentence that happened first. Write 2 next to the sentence that happened second. Then write one sentence. Use the past time clause in parentheses.

1. The scientist retired. _1_
   He began research on a new area of interest. _2_

   (before) The scientist had retired before he began research on a new area of interest.

2. I didn't know about the research. _2_
   I heard the podcast. _1_

   (until) _but_ _____

3. It started to rain. ___ ²
   We finished hiking. ___ ¹
   (before) _had_ _____

4. Mari picked up the phone. _2_
   It stopped ringing. _2_ |
   (by the time) _____

5. My sister _had_ told me. _2_
   I didn't realize my sweater was on backwards. _1_
   (until) _____

6. Nawaf _had_ left his house. _2_
   His mother called. _1_
   (when) _____

7. I drank the cup of coffee. ___
   I realized it wasn't mine. ___
   (before) _____

8. We arrived at the airport. ___
   Our plane departed. ___
   (by the time) _____

B. APPLY Complete the sentences with information that is true for you. Then take turns reading your sentences with a partner.

1. I _had realized my mother isn't home_ when I got home yesterday.
2. I _had realized that this class is Chinese class_ until I started taking this class.
3. I _had turned 18 yo_ by the time I graduated from high school.
4. I _had married_ by the year 2000.
5. I _hadn't concentrated on class_ before I _finished class_.

iQ PRACTICE Go online for more practice using the past perfect.
Practice > Unit 5 > Activity 11

iQ PRACTICE Go online for the Grammar Expansion: past perfect continuous.
Practice > Unit 5 > Activity 12.

The contraction **'d** is frequently used instead of *had* in affirmative statements with the past perfect. Noticing *had* and the contraction **'d** can help you better understand the order of past events.

Listen to these examples. The speaker joins **'d** to words that follow beginning with vowel sounds and certain consonant sounds (*l, r*). Notice that **'d** is not stressed.

> I**'d** already finished the test when the teacher collected our papers.
>
> He**'d** eaten at that restaurant before.
>
> We**'d** often talked about getting married.
>
> You**'d** left when we got there.
>
> She**'d** written her email before she received mine.

Do not use a contraction with questions. Notice that *had* is not stressed in these questions.

> **Had** you heard from him by the time you left?
>
> **Had** everyone finished the test by 2:00?

The contraction with negatives is *hadn't*.

> I **hadn't** finished my phone call by the time the train arrived.
>
> They **hadn't** gone to the mall before they ate dinner.

A. IDENTIFY Listen to the sentences. Check (✓) the sentence you hear.

1. ☐ He worked at a bookstore.
   ☑ He'd worked at a bookstore.

2. ☑ We left when it started raining.
   ☐ We'd left when it started raining.

3. ☑ They answered the questions.
   ☐ They'd answered the questions.

4. ☑ I've eaten my lunch.
   ☐ I'd eaten my lunch.

5. ☐ You've already taken the test.
   ☑ You'd already taken the test.

6. ☐ She didn't work there.
   ☑ She hadn't worked there.

7. ☑ It hasn't started to rain.
   ☐ It hadn't started to rain.

8. ☐ Has he found it?
   ☑ Had he found it?

9. ☑ Have you called Alex?
   ☐ Had you called Alex?

B. IDENTIFY Listen again. Repeat the sentences. Then take turns saying and identifying the sentences from Activity A with a partner.

iQ PRACTICE Go online for more practice with the contraction of *had*.
Practice > Unit 5 > Activity 13

When you give a short presentation in class or at work, start by introducing your topic clearly.

Here are some phrases you can use to introduce your topic.

I want to talk about . . .

My topic is . . .

This presentation is on . . .

I'm going to talk about . . .

During your presentation, it is important to use words and phrases that help your audience understand the order of events and the reasons for them.

Here are some words and phrases you can use to help your audience follow and understand your presentation.

Order of events	Purpose/reason
First,	so . . .
Second,	so that . . .
After that,	in order to . . .
Then,	The reason I took this risk was . . .
Before	
By the time	

A. IDENTIFY Listen to this presentation. Complete the sentences with the words and phrases you hear.

LEARNING JAPANESE

_____I'm going to Talkabout__ a time I took a risk and it
(1)

turned out well. I'd always wanted to learn to speak Japanese.

When I was in high school, I started to take classes in Japanese.

____By The time____ I graduated from college, I had
(2)

studied the language for eight years, but I still couldn't speak it very

well, _____So_____ I decided to go to Japan to
(3)

study. I didn't know anyone there. My grandmother had given me

money the year before, _____So_____ I used that
(4)

for the trip. _____Before_____ I left, I'd done some
(5)

research on language schools. I stayed in Japan for three months

and met some great people there. My Japanese improved a lot.

_____By the time_____ I finally returned to my country, I had
(6)

become fluent.

TIP FOR SUCCESS

When listening, make sure you maintain eye contact. This encourages the speaker and shows that you are interested.

B. CATEGORIZE Check (✓) the risks you would take to learn English. Add some of your own ideas.

☐ join a club or sports team where people speak English

☐ take classes in other subjects with native English speakers

☐ move to a new city or country

☐ meet and talk to native speakers

☐ travel in English-speaking countries

☐ (your idea) _____

☐ (your idea) _____

C. DISCUSS Work with a partner. Take turns talking about the risks you checked in Activity B. Use words and phrases from the Speaking Skill box on page 120.

iQ PRACTICE Go online for more practice giving a short presentation.
Practice > Unit 5 > Activity 14

UNIT ASSIGNMENT
OBJECTIVE ▶

Give a short presentation

In this assignment, you are going to give a one-minute presentation on a risk you have taken. As you prepare your presentation, think about the Unit Question, "Does taking risks change our lives?" Use information from Listening 1, Listening 2, the unit video, and your work in this unit to support your presentation. Refer to the Self-Assessment checklist on page 124.

[handwritten notes in left margin:]
for
· back packing

· MB → house
- (friend)

working → needa
leave

move
wanted to change
Italy - where? place
to

· worth taking
This movie is worth watching

· give in

· work out
understand.

· destiny

· make up
my mind
↳ decide.

CONSIDER THE IDEAS

INVESTIGATE Listen to one man talk about a risk he took and the reasons why he took it. Take notes as you listen. Then discuss the questions with a partner.

1. What had his life been like before? *Normal, good house - good job.*

2. What did he risk by leaving? *give up everything*

3. Do you think it was a good risk to take? Why or why not?

4. What do you think happened when he arrived in Rome? *best experience* *He met*

PREPARE AND SPEAK

A. GATHER IDEAS Think about the experience of the speaker in the Consider the Ideas activity above. Have you had a similar experience? What risks in your own life do you feel were good to take? Make a list.

_____

_____

_____

B. ORGANIZE IDEAS Choose one risk from your list in Activity A. Prepare to talk about it. Use the outline to help you organize your ideas.

The risk you took: _____bought my car_____

The reason why you took this risk:

_____

_____

_____

_____

_____

Describe what happened:

_____

_____

_____

_____

_____

_____

_____

_____

_____

What did you learn or gain from this experience?

_____

_____

_____

_____

_____

_____

C. SPEAK Give a one-minute presentation to your group or class about a risk you have taken. Use your notes from Activities A and B. Refer to the Self-Assessment checklist below before you begin.

1. Use an appropriate phrase to introduce your topic.

2. Use your notes from Activity B to help you, but do not read exactly what you wrote.

3. Try to talk continuously for the entire minute.

iQ PRACTICE Go online for your alternate Unit Assignment.
Practice > Unit 5 > Activity 15

CHECK AND REFLECT

A. CHECK Think about the Unit Assignment as you complete the Self-Assessment checklist.

SELF-ASSESSMENT	Yes	No
I was able to speak easily about the topic.	☐	☐
My group or class understood me.	☐	☐
I used vocabulary from the unit.	☐	☐
I used the past perfect and simple past.	☐	☐
I used contractions of *had*.	☐	☐
I used phrases to introduce my topic, explain the order of events, and give reasons for events.	☐	☐

B. REFLECT Discuss these questions with a partner or group.

1. What is something new you learned in this unit?

2. Look back at the Unit Question—Does taking risks change our lives? Is your answer different now than when you started this unit? If yes, how is it different? Why?

iQ PRACTICE Go to the online discussion board to discuss the questions.
Practice > Unit 5 > Activity 16

TRACK YOUR SUCCESS

iQ PRACTICE Go online to check the words and phrases you have learned in this unit. *Practice > Unit 5 > Activity 17*

Check (✓) the skills you learned. If you need more work on a skill, refer to the page(s) in parentheses.

NOTE-TAKING	☐ I can use a chart to separate risks and outcomes. (p. 102)
LISTENING	☐ I can listen for different kinds of numbers. (p. 103)
CRITICAL THINKING	☐ I can evaluate the strength and relevance of evidence. (pp. 107–108)
VOCABULARY	☐ I can use word families. (p. 115)
GRAMMAR	☐ I can use the past perfect. (p. 117)
PRONUNCIATION	☐ I can use contractions of *had*. (p. 119)
SPEAKING	☐ I can give a short presentation. (p. 120)
OBJECTIVE ▶	☐ I can gather information and ideas to give a short presentation on a risk I have taken.

6 Neurology

Will artificial intelligence ever be as smart as humans?

A. Discuss these questions with your classmates.

1. What does "artificial intelligence" (AI) mean?

2. Give some examples of things in your daily life that use AI.

3. Look at the photo. What kind of machine is this? Where are the people?

B. Listen to *The Q Classroom* online. Then answer these questions.

1. What does Yuna assume when she buys an electronic device? Do you ever do the same?

2. How does Felix feel about the use of AI in so many places?

3. How does Sophy feel about electronic devices? Do you feel the same or differently? Explain.

iQ PRACTICE Go to the online discussion board to discuss the Unit Question with your classmates. *Practice > Unit 6 > Activity 1*

UNIT OBJECTIVE

Listen to a radio interview and an excerpt from a college class discussion. Gather information and ideas to state and explain your opinions in a group discussion about research into artificial intelligence.

LISTENING 1

What Kind of "Smart" Is AI?

OBJECTIVE ▶

You are going to listen to a radio interview with two experts in artificial intelligence. As you listen to the interview, gather information and ideas about whether AI will ever be as smart as humans.

PREVIEW THE LISTENING

A. PREVIEW The interviewer's first question is, "So, are machines now as smart as we are?" What do you think? Discuss your ideas with a partner. Take notes on your discussion.

B. VOCABULARY Read aloud these words from Listening 1. Check (✓) the ones you know. Use a dictionary to define any new or unknown words. Then discuss with a partner how the words will relate to the unit.

automated (adj.)	**layer** (n.) 🔑	**reject** (v.) 🔑 OPAL
clever (adj.) 🔑	**obvious** (adj.) 🔑 OPAL	**stand by** (v. phr.)
fair (adj.) 🔑	**predictable** (adj.)	**take over** (v. phr.)
figure out (v. phr.)		

🔑 Oxford 3000™ words   **OPAL** Oxford Phrasal Academic Lexicon

iQ PRACTICE Go online to listen and practice your pronunciation.
Practice > Unit 6 > Activity 2

WORK WITH THE LISTENING

A. LISTEN AND TAKE NOTES Listen to the radio interview. As you listen, complete the notes.

iQ RESOURCES Go online to download extra vocabulary support.
Resources > Extra Vocabulary > Unit 6

Concerns about using robots

AI = _Artificial intelligent_ *go mean no made*

— VanDyke: Is AI smarter? depends on _what_ by smart

— Ngoma: Old tasks (e.g., moon landings and remembering *phonenumber*
phonenumber) isn't being "smart"

Some jobs AI might take over soon:

(1) driving _and truck_ —10 years

(2) writing _best seller novel_ —30 years

(3) performing _surgelly_ —40 years

Why?

(1) most jobs are _~~taken~~ routine_

(2) people eventually accept machines—e.g., laser _eye surgolly_

(3) machines do jobs better, more cheaply

AI Trucks:

— suitable because truck driving mostly _predictable_

— BUT: First and last _miles_ need humans because
too many unpredictable things on streets

— Two layers of information for AI trucks:

· _GPS_ system

· sets of _sensor_

AI Hacking:

— Some targets: *power*

· electric _~~traffic~~_ system

· _banking_ system

— Ngoma: Dangerous but many experts working on _security_

B. CATEGORIZE Read the statements. Write *T* (true) or *F* (false) according to what the interviewer and his two guests say. Then correct each false statement to make it true.

_____ 1. Machines can make wise decisions, just as humans can.

_____ 2. Experts predict that AI will take over medical surgery before it takes over writing a novel.

_____ 3. Most laser eye surgery is now automated.

_____ 4. Driving a car around town is less predictable than driving a truck on the highway.

_____ 5. An AI-controlled truck is a kind of robot.

_____ 6. AI trucks have more trouble with GPS systems than with their sensors.

C. IDENTIFY Read the sentences. Then listen again. Circle the answer that best completes each statement.

1. Dr. Ngoma says that most people no longer consider _____ a sign that AI is smart.

   a. storing a lot information

   b. choosing how to use information

2. Dr. VanDyke implies that AI might take over jobs _____ than experts predict.

   a. more quickly

   b. more slowly

3. Dr. VanDyke suggests that 30 years ago people did not _____.

   a. believe they could get eye surgery

   b. consider automated eye surgery safe

4. Dr. Ngoma says that for the first and last mile of a truck trip, _____.

   a. humans should drive the trucks

   b. city streets should be redesigned

5. The interviewer says many people are worried that criminals will use AI to _____.

   a. steal trucks and cause accidents

   b. damage basic systems that keep society running

In Unit 4, you learned about using context clues to identify the meaning of words. Remember to read the whole sentence and consider the **context**. This can help you identify the correct word (or phrase) and meaning.

D. VOCABULARY Use the new vocabulary from Listening 1. Complete each sentence with the correct word or phrase.

automated *(adj.)*	figure out *(v. phr.)*	predictable *(adj.)*	stand by *(v. phr.)*
clever *(adj.)*	layer *(n.)*	reject *(v.)*	take over *(v. phr.)*
fair *(adj.)*	obvious *(adj.)*		

1. Each window is made of three _____: one of glass, one of clear plastic, and another of glass.

2. The judge made a(n) _____ decision about dividing up the money. Each person got an equal share.

3. I washed my car at a(n) _____ car wash because it's faster than washing it by hand.

4. After the team fell behind by five goals, it was _____ that they were going to lose.

5. The owners of this company don't run it well. I wish some larger company would _____ the operation.

6. The movie had a very _____ plot: Two people fall in love, they have a fight, and then in the end, they get back together. I knew that would happen.

7. Dolphins are known to be very _____ animals. They've even been seen using tools!

8. Todd has never run this machine before. I think I will _____ just in case he needs help.

9. Young people may _____ traditions and then, when they get older, return to the old ways.

10. You never told me you were planning to quit, but it wasn't difficult to _____ from the way you were acting.

iQ PRACTICE Go online for more practice with the vocabulary.
Practice > Unit 6 > Activity 3

iQ PRACTICE Go online for additional listening and comprehension.
Practice > Unit 6 > Activity 4

? SAY WHAT YOU THINK

DISCUSS Discuss the questions in a group.

1. Are some AI systems truly smart? After hearing the interview about AI, what do you think?

2. If AI systems take over a lot of jobs from humans, will that be a good thing?

LISTENING SKILL Inferring a speaker's attitude

You can learn a lot about **a speaker's attitude** by noticing the way he or she talks. Someone who speaks slowly or sometimes hesitates before speaking might be nervous. Someone who raises his or her voice could be angry. Someone who is bored or uninterested might speak in a low voice with level intonation.

Listen to this excerpt from the radio show. Notice that the interviewer changes his tone and emphasizes some words. This indicates that he feels strongly about the topic and is perhaps a little worried.

> Think of everything else that is under AI control—our electric power system, the city water systems, the banking system, air traffic—wow!

Listen to this conversation. Notice that Speaker A speaks in a low voice with level intonation, expressing a lack of interest. Speaker B speaks slowly and hesitates. This shows he is nervous.

> **A:** It's the neighbor again. What does he want this time?
>
> **B:** Excuse me. Would you mind turning down the TV, please?
>
> **A:** Yeah, sure.

A. IDENTIFY Listen to these sentences. Match each sentence with the speaker's attitude.

_____ 1. Did you know that this is a nonsmoking area?   a. uninterested

_____ 2. I don't know why Simon's always late for work.   b. angry

_____ 3. Yeah. That garbage has been there for a week.   c. nervous

B. IDENTIFY Listen to each conversation. Check (✓) the word that describes how the woman feels.

1. ☐ uninterested ☑ angry ☐ nervous

2. ☐ uninterested ☐ angry ☑ nervous

3. ☑ uninterested ☐ angry ☐ nervous

C. APPLY Work with a partner. Take turns reading the sentences. Practice sounding angry, uninterested, or nervous. Your partner will try to identify how you feel.

1. Someone's left the front door open again.

2. I think there's something wrong with the engine.

3. Muna hasn't finished the report yet.

iQ PRACTICE Go online for more practice inferring a speaker's attitude. *Practice > Unit 6 > Activity 5*

TIP FOR SUCCESS
In discussion activities, always try to use words you have studied in the unit. This will help you learn the words and remember them in the future.

LISTENING 2

Asking the Right Questions about AI

OBJECTIVE ▶

You are going to listen to an excerpt from a college class discussion. As you listen to the excerpt, gather information and ideas about whether AI will ever be as smart as humans.

PREVIEW THE LISTENING

A. PREVIEW The students are discussing the issue of how to evaluate AI in relation to the human brain. Before you listen, think about your encounters in everyday life with AI "personalities," such as cell phone "assistants." Note your ideas, and then share them with the class.

B. VOCABULARY Read aloud these words from Listening 2. Check (✓) the ones you know. Use a dictionary to define any new or unknown words. Then discuss with a partner how the words will relate to the unit.

be supposed to (do something) *(v. phr.)*	in this case *(adv. phr.)* OPAL
celebrity *(n.)* 🔑	keep up with *(v. phr.)*
companion *(n.)*	landscape *(n.)* 🔑
criterion *(n.)* 🔑 OPAL	program *(v.)* 🔑 OPAL
genius *(n.)*	take sides *(v. phr.)*

🔑 Oxford 3000™ words

OPAL Oxford Phrasal Academic Lexicon

iQ PRACTICE Go online to listen and practice your pronunciation.
Practice > Unit 6 > Activity 7

WORK WITH THE LISTENING

A. LISTEN AND TAKE NOTES Listen to the classroom discussion about AI and humans. Take a few notes about each of the following topics.

- Review of last week

- Picture 1

- Picture 2

- Comparison of two objects

iQ RESOURCES Go online to download extra vocabulary support.
Resources > Extra Vocabulary > Unit 6

Picture 1   Picture 2

B. IDENTIFY Listen again to the class discussion. Circle the answer that best completes each statement.

1. In an earlier class, the students had learned not to ask whether AI or humans were smarter because the answer is always: _____ a _____ .

   a. it depends on what one means by "smart"

   b. AI cannot possibly match humans

   c. humans can't manage as much information as AI

ACADEMIC LANGUAGE

The corpus shows that speakers use *is important to . . .* to draw attention to something. The lecturer in Listening 2 uses this phrase to draw attention to why Alan Turing created the Turing Test.

_____ **OPAL**
Oxford Phrasal Academic Lexicon

2. The students and professor make a few mistakes _____ c _____ .

   a. in remembering whether Sophia is a woman or a robot

   b. in deciding whether Sophia is good or bad

   c. in using the correct pronoun to refer to Sophia

3. One thing Sophia is famous for is _____ c _____ .

   a. being smarter than any other AI device

   b. having a real human body

   c. being named a citizen of a real country

4. One purpose of social robots is to _____ b _____ .

   a. spend time with and talk to people in places like hospitals

   b. learn to play games like chess better than human champions

   c. solve difficult problems between countries and prevent wars

5. One of the Curiosity rover's jobs is to _____ a _____ .

   a. collect samples on Mars

   b. look and sound human

   c. make maps of Earth by observing from Mars

6. According to the professor, NASA scientists think Curiosity _____ b _____ .

   a. should be replaced

   b. is not as tough as it should be

   c. is as smart as it needs to be

7. In order to _____ a _____ , the professor mentions that Sophia said she wants to destroy humans.

   a. show that robots like Sophia are dangerous

   b. support the point that Sophia makes mistakes

   c. indicate that Sophia's maker has lost control of it

8. To pass the Turing Test, an AI device must make a human _____.

    a. believe that it is human

    b. think it looks like a human

    c. live a more productive life

CRITICAL THINKING STRATEGY

Justifying claims

When you **justify** claims, you give support for them. You offer reasons or evidence to convince someone to accept your claim. Sometimes, factual supporting details are a good way to justify a claim. At other times, you justify your claims by saying what makes sense or explaining how the claim fits in with principles that you and the listener consider right.

Here are some useful expressions for justifying claims.

For Justifying Claims with Facts	For Justifying Claims with Reasons
Research/Studies have shown . . .	My main reason is . . .
Scientists/Experts have discovered . . .	It makes sense that . . .
A lot of evidence suggests . . .	It's important to remember (that) . . .
Actually, / In fact, . . .	A big consideration is . . .

iQ PRACTICE   Go online to watch the Critical Thinking Video and check your comprehension. *Practice > Unit 6 > Activity 6*

C. APPLY Work with a partner. Here are some claims related to the class discussion about comparing AI and humans. Take turns justifying the claims. Use expressions from the box above in your justifications.

1. The robot called Sophia is a celebrity.

2. The AI-to-human comparison is important in the case of Sophia.

3. The rover Curiosity does more real work than Sophia.

4. NASA doesn't consider Curiosity a genius.

5. Conversation requires a lot of intelligence.

6. The question "Can machines think?" gets muddled up by different definitions.

D. DISCUSS Discuss the questions in a group.

1. The social robot Sophia was declared a citizen of a real country. Should AI devices become "citizens," with all the legal rights that human citizens have? Why or why not?

2. Do you think it's valuable to have social robots like Sophia? Why or why not?

E. VOCABULARY Use the new vocabulary from Listening 2. Read the sentences. Then match each bold word with the correct definition.

____ 1. With so many entertainment media, it's easier now for someone to become a **celebrity**.

____ 2. A pet like a parrot can be a good **companion** for a disabled person who lives alone.

____ 3. The law says that being 35 years old is one **criterion** for becoming president.

____ 4. In my opinion, a **genius** can see connections among ideas that other people can't see.

____ 5. There are many reasons for moving. **In this case**, the family wanted to live closer to relatives.

____ 6. I get so many email messages every day that I can't really **keep up with** them.

____ 7. The **landscape** in this part of the state is hilly and forested, unlike the flatter area down south.

____ 8. In this computer science class, students will learn how to **program** games and animations.

____ 9. Schools **are supposed to** give you enough knowledge to fully participate in society.

____ 10. I tried to stay out of the argument, but I had to **take sides** when one of the people started telling lies about me.

a. *(v. phr.)* be believed or expected to be/do something

b. *(n.)* a famous person

c. *(adv. phr.)* in this set of conditions

d. *(n.)* everything you can see when you look across a large area of land

e. *(v. phr.)* to express support for somebody in a disagreement

f. *(n.)* someone who stays near to another much of the time

g. *(v.)* to give a computer a set of instructions to make it do a task

h. *(v.)* to learn about or be aware of the latest information regarding something

i. *(n.)* an extremely smart person

j. *(n.)* a standard or principle by which something is judged

iQ PRACTICE   Go online for more practice with the vocabulary.
Practice ⟩ Unit 6 ⟩ Activity 8

WORK WITH THE VIDEO

A. PREVIEW What do you know about the development of artificial intelligence?

VIDEO VOCABULARY

logic (*n.*) the use of reason or good sense

conceive of (*v.*) to come up with the idea to build or establish something

theoretical (*adj.*) based on ideas about something but not necessarily really in existence

algorithm (*n.*) a set of steps for achieving an outcome

Alan Turing

iQ RESOURCES Go online to watch the video about Alan Turing.
Resources > Video > Unit 6 > Unit Video

B. JUSTIFY Watch the video two or three times. Listen for the claims listed in the chart below. Complete the notes about the justification(s) in the video for each claim. Note: A justification may not occur immediately after the claim but later in the video.

Claim	Justification from the video
The death of a friend influenced Turing's thinking.	After his friend's death, Turing _____.
The Universal Turing Machine was a great theoretical accomplishment.	If the machine had been built, it could have _____.
By the standards of the Turing Test, true artificial intelligence has not yet been achieved.	No machine has yet been able to _____.
Turing has achieved a kind of immortality.	Even after his death, his ideas continue to _____.

C. EXTEND How do Turing's ideas relate to the unit question, "Will artificial intelligence ever be as smart as humans?" Discuss with a partner.

SAY WHAT YOU THINK

SYNTHESIZE Think about the unit video, Listening 1, and Listening 2 as you discuss the questions.

1. Are we moving too fast in turning tasks over to AI devices? Are there dangers in letting AI take over certain things? Explain.

2. Will AI devices ever become truly more intelligent than the human brain? Justify your answer.

VOCABULARY SKILL Using the dictionary

Finding the correct meaning

Words listed in a dictionary often have several meanings. To choose the correct meaning, first identify the part of speech (*noun, verb, adjective,* etc.). Then read all the definitions and example sentences. Finally, choose the meaning that best matches the context.

For example, read this conversation.

> **Nour:** Look, May. I found this gold ring in the park. It fits me perfectly!
>
> **May:** You're not going to keep it, are you? That's wrong! Turn it in to the police.

W*rong* can be a verb, a noun, an adjective, or an adverb. Here, *wrong* is an adjective. W*rong (adj.)* in this dictionary entry has four different meanings. By considering the context and comparing examples, you will find that the most appropriate definition is Number 4—"not good or right."

> **wrong**¹ ⚲ /rɔŋ/ *adj.* **1** not true or not correct; not right: *the wrong answer* ◆ *You have the wrong number* (= on the telephone). ◆ *I think you're wrong about that.* **ANT right 2** not the best; not suitable: *That's the wrong way to hold the bat.* ◆ *I think she married the wrong man.* **ANT right 3** (not before a noun) **wrong (with sb/sth)** causing problems or difficulties; not as it should be: *You look upset. Is something wrong?* ◆ ***What's wrong** with the car this time?* ◆ *She has something wrong with her leg.* **4 wrong (to do sth)** bad or against the law; not good or right: *It's wrong to tell lies.* ◆ *The man said that he had done nothing wrong.*

All dictionary entries adapted from the *Oxford American Dictionary for learners of English* © Oxford University Press 2011

A. EXPLAIN Read the sentences. Use a dictionary. Follow the steps in the Vocabulary Skill box on page 139 to identify the correct meaning of each bold word. Then write the definition.

1. People living in a **just** society should respect the law.

   (adjective) fair and right; reasonable

2. Complaints against dishonest politicians have reached a **peak** in the last few years.

   _____

3. In any relationship, it's important to be **open** and supportive.

   _____

4. I don't have **outstanding** bills. I paid them all on Wednesday.

   _____

5. People in positions of authority shouldn't **abuse** their power.

   _____

6. Terri lives a very **moral** life. She's a good example for her children.

   _____

7. Companies that continue to pollute the environment **risk** getting heavy fines.

   _____

8. If it doesn't stop raining soon, I think we should **abandon** the idea of going for a walk.

   _____

B. CREATE Choose five words from Activity A and write your own sentences. Then compare your sentences with a partner.

iQ PRACTICE Go online for more practice using the dictionary.
Practice › Unit 6 › Activity 9

SPEAKING

OBJECTIVE ▶ At the end of this unit, you will take part in a group discussion. Make sure to take turns leading the group discussion.

GRAMMAR Gerunds and infinitives as the objects of verbs

A **gerund** is **the base form of the verb + -*ing***. Gerunds can be used as the objects of certain verbs, e.g., *admit, avoid, discuss, dislike, enjoy, finish, miss, quit*.

⌈ Nigel enjoys **doing** the chores.
⌊ After she left home, Emily missed **seeing** her family.

An **infinitive** is *to* + **the base form of the verb**. Infinitives can also be used as the objects of certain verbs, e.g., *agree, choose, decide, hope, learn, need, plan, want*.

⌈ Managers decided **to ignore** the public's concerns about automated cars.
⌊ The company plans **to increase** its use of robots by 10 percent over the next year.

Some verbs can be followed by either a gerund or an infinitive, with no difference in meaning, e.g., *begin, hate, like, love, prefer*.

⌈ Workers at the factory began **demanding** promises of job security.
⌊ Workers at the factory began **to demand** promises of job security.

A. APPLY Circle the correct verb forms to complete the conversation. If both the infinitive and the gerund are possible, circle both answers. Then practice the conversation with a partner.

Vicky: Hey, Janice. I just heard that the company has decided (giving / to give)
1
everybody one of those wireless smart speakers next month.

Janice: OK. That's nice. I enjoy (having / to have) a little music while I work.
2

Vicky: Well, music is not the point. They hope (getting / to get) us to use them
3
as part of the so-called smart office.

Janice: I have no idea what you mean.

Vicky: The bosses want (changing / to change) our habits so we'll be more
4
efficient. They think it will happen if we use the speakers like assistants. "Hey, speaker, turn off my desk light." That kind of thing.

Janice: Is that why they've begun (putting / to put) sensors on all the lights and
5
the thermostats and the copier and everything?

Vicky: That's right. So the copier will basically be asleep most of the time. If you want (copying / to copy) something, you tell your speaker, it wakes up the copier, and then your copies are made.

<u>6</u>

Janice: AI to the rescue, right? But what if I prefer (doing / to do) things the old way, by hand?

<u>7</u>

Vicky: Too bad, my friend. You can choose (being / to be) a part of the smart office, or you can lose the ability to turn on the lights or the coffee maker.

<u>8</u>

B. CREATE Answer the questions. Use the bold words in your answers. Then discuss your answers with a partner and identify the gerunds and infinitives you and your partner used.

1. Which activities or tasks do we absolutely **need** to use AI devices for—things that cannot be done without AI?

2. What AI-related activities do you **like** doing? Are there any activities that you **dislike** using AI devices for?

3. Consider the possible dangers of widespread use of AI. What should societies **avoid** using AI for?

4. Some people have **decided** to **quit** using AI devices in some situations—e.g., posting to social media, using GPS maps, and doing banking online. Does such a decision make sense? Why or why not?

iQ PRACTICE Go online for more practice with gerunds and infinitives.
Practice > Unit 6 > Activities 10–11

PRONUNCIATION Stress on important words

Speakers usually put more **stress** on the important words in a sentence, such as nouns, verbs, adjectives, and adverbs. These words are usually louder and clearer than other words in the sentence. Listening for stressed words can help you hear and understand the most important information.

Listen to this excerpt from Listening 1. Notice how the speaker stresses the important words.

I think a **lot** of people are **afraid** that **hackers** can take **over** AI systems. And **not** just that someone might take **over** a truck's **controls**. **Think** of everything **else** that is under AI **control**—our electric **power** system, the city **water** systems, the **banking** system, **air traffic** . . .

iQ RESOURCES Go online to watch the Pronunciation Skill Video.
Resources > Video > Unit 6 > Pronunciation Skill Video

A. IDENTIFY Listen to more sentences from Listening 1. Underline the stressed words.

1. You and I can choose how to use those equations or phone numbers wisely.

2. Apparently, a survey asked experts in AI to predict how soon machines could do certain jobs better and more cheaply than humans.

3. Of course, very powerful machines with enough information can do things that even seem creative to us.

4. The second layer comes from a set of sensors—little devices kind of like cameras that "read" the details of its environment.

5. But the good news is that many very smart AI experts specialize in security, and they are dedicated professionals.

 B. APPLY Listen again. Repeat the sentences. Practice stressing the important words.

iQ PRACTICE Go online for more practice with word stress.
Practice > Unit 6 > Activity 12

SPEAKING SKILL Leading a group discussion

When discussing a topic in a group, it is important to choose one person to **lead the discussion**. The role of the leader is to guide the flow of the discussion. The leader:

- starts the discussion,

- gets comments from the members of the group,

- keeps the discussion on topic, and

- ends the discussion.

Here are some phrases you can use when you are leading a discussion.

Starting the discussion

☐ Today we're going to discuss . . .   Our topic today is . . .

Getting comments from different people

☐ What do you think, Reza?   Lin, what's your opinion?
 Do you have anything to add, Jon?

Keeping on topic

☐ Sorry, but can we keep to the topic?   Let's get back on topic.

Ending the discussion

☐ That's all we have time for today.   To sum up, then, . . . (summarize)

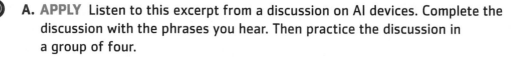

A. APPLY Listen to this excerpt from a discussion on AI devices. Complete the discussion with the phrases you hear. Then practice the discussion in a group of four.

Leader: OK, so today _____ the recent boom in AI devices

for everyday tasks. Are AI toasters and electric shavers a good thing, or a waste of

money? Brad, _____?

Brad: Well, they might not be totally necessary, but I don't see any harm in them. If people want to waste their money, that's their business.

Leader: OK. _____, Seline?

Seline: I don't agree. They might be harmful in some ways. It's not good for people to do everything through a cell phone. And the more you depend on electronics, the less exercise you get.

Brad: I get a lot of exercise. I run three miles a day and . . .

Leader: Sorry, but _____? Susan, _____?

Susan: Well, I probably agree with Seline. Every AI device can be hacked. There are cases where criminals have broken into computer systems by going through coffee makers or rice cookers.

Leader: OK, so _____, Susan and Seline feel the spread of AI devices is not good, while Brad thinks there's nothing wrong with it.

B. EXTEND Work with a partner. Continue the discussion from Activity A, using your own ideas.

iQ PRACTICE Go online for more practice leading a group discussion.
Practice > Unit 6 > Activity 13

NOTE-TAKING SKILL Building an outline to take notes on a discussion

Building an outline is an effective way to take notes on a discussion. An outline is useful if you need to take comprehensive notes, as it will help you to make sure you cover all the main topics and ideas. It will also show you how the different topics and ideas relate to each other, as well as allow you to record examples and other supporting details in a systematic way.

To organize your notes in outline form, list the main topics or ideas and then use indentation to record supporting details.

A. ANALYZE Study this outline from the discussion about AI devices between Brad, Susan, and Seline. Notice how the main topics or ideas of their discussion are noted, along with their supporting ideas.

Topic: Is the increase in AI devices a good thing?

(main point) Increase is OK

(opinion) The devices don't harm anything.

(opinion) People have a right to waste their money if they like.

(main point) Having too many devices can be harmful.

(opinion) not good to operate everything through a phone

(supporting idea) keeps people from getting exercise

(opinion) danger from hacking AI devices

(supporting idea) computer systems have been hacked

through AI appliances

B. EXTEND With a partner, think back to your discussion on AI devices in Activity B on page 142. Add any additional ideas and supporting details to the outline above.

C. IDENTIFY Listen again to Listening 2. Complete this outline on the discussion.

Asking the Right Questions about Artificial Intelligence

(main topic) Questions from previous discussion

      (detail) Does AI = human intelligence? Don't ask; answer always similar + different

      (detail) Why do we want to compare _____ and AI?

(main topic) Social robot Sophia

      (detail) looks like _____ but with metal instead of hair

      (detail) famous; declared a _____ of Saudi Arabia

      (detail) purpose = eventually be _____, do customer service, etc.

(main topic) Mars rover Curiosity

      (detail) does not look human

      (detail) does its job (collecting _____) without interacting with humans

(main topic) Comparing the intelligence of Curiosity and Sophia

      (detail) Curiosity not as "smart" as a 2012 _____.

      (detail) Curiosity very _____ instead

      (detail) Sophia's tasks require more complicated intelligence

      (detail) Sophia still makes a lot of _____.

(main topic) ? Turing Test

      (detail) Description of test—AI to convince human that _____

      (detail) Sophia would probably not pass.

iQ PRACTICE Go online for more practice building an outline to take notes on a discussion. *Practice > Unit 6 > Activity 14*

UNIT ASSIGNMENT Take part in a group discussion

OBJECTIVE ▶

In this assignment, you are going to take part in a group discussion. As you prepare for the group discussion, think about the Unit Question, "Will artificial intelligence ever be as smart as humans?" Use information from Listening 1, Listening 2, the unit video, and your work in this unit to support your discussion. Refer to the Self-Assessment checklist on page 148.

CONSIDER THE IDEAS

EXTEND Work in a group. Make a list of issues related to the intelligence of AI as compared to human intelligence. List reasons why you think AI can be smarter than humans or reasons why it can't.

_____

_____

_____

_____

PREPARE AND SPEAK

A. GATHER IDEAS Read the statements. Check (✓) the ones you agree with.

☐ The human brain has a flexibility and adaptability that AI can never match.

☐ Humans make AI devices, and it is impossible for the AI to be smarter than its maker.

☐ AI devices can learn from their experiences and surroundings.

☐ AI devices are already smarter than humans in some ways.

☐ AI devices cannot really understand humans.

☐ If AI devices look and speak a lot like humans, humans will feel friendship toward them.

☐ AI devices that pass the Turing Test are truly intelligent.

B. ORGANIZE IDEAS Choose two statements from Activity A that you agree with and one that you disagree with. Write or record each statement and label it *agree* or *disagree*. Then list reasons that support your opinion of each statement. Create an outline to help you prepare to give your opinion and justify it.

TIP FOR SUCCESS

When taking part in a group discussion, encourage other speakers by paying close attention. You might also want to take notes of any good ideas.

C. SPEAK Have a group discussion about whether or not AI devices can ever be as smart as humans. Refer to the Self-Assessment checklist below before you begin.

1. Choose a leader for your discussion. The leader can begin the discussion by asking about your responses to the statements in Activity A.

2. When an issue you have written about in Activity B comes up for discussion, state your ideas or opinions and justify these claims.

3. You can refer to your notes, but do not read exactly what you wrote.

4. Give each student a turn as group leader.

iQ PRACTICE Go online for your alternate Unit Assignment.
Practice > Unit 6 > Activity 15

CHECK AND REFLECT

A. CHECK Think about the Unit Assignment as you complete the Self-Assessment checklist.

SELF-ASSESSMENT	Yes	No
I was able to speak easily about the topic.	☐	☐
My group understood me.	☐	☐
I used vocabulary from the unit.	☐	☐
I put stress on important words as I spoke.	☐	☐
I led a group discussion.	☐	☐
I used an outline to take notes on the discussion.	☐	☐
I justified the claims I made.	☐	☐

B. REFLECT Discuss these questions with a partner or group.

1. What is something new you learned in this unit?

2. Look back at the Unit Question—Will artificial intelligence ever be as smart as humans? Is your answer different now than when you started this unit? If yes, how is it different? Why?

iQ PRACTICE Go to the online discussion board to discuss the questions.
Practice > Unit 6 > Activity 16

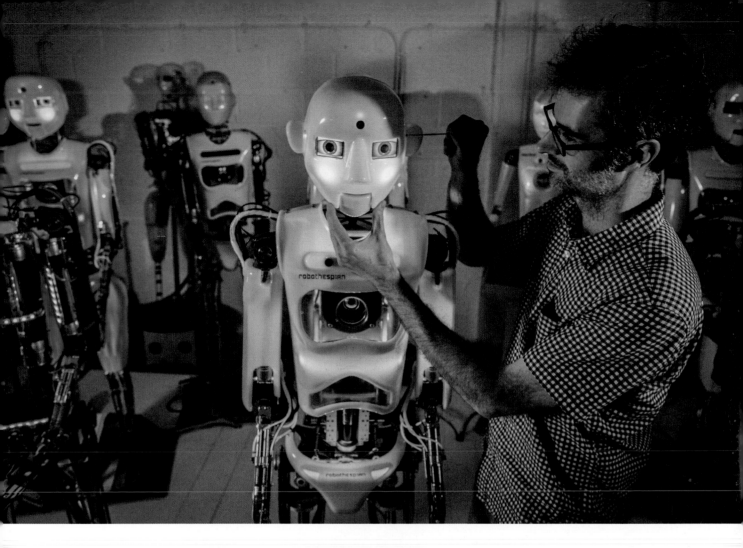

TRACK YOUR SUCCESS

iQ PRACTICE Go online to check the words and phrases you have learned in this unit. *Practice > Unit 6 > Activity 17*

Check (✓) the skills you learned. If you need more work on a skill, refer to the page(s) in parentheses.

LISTENING   ☐ I can infer a speaker's attitude. (p. 132)

CRITICAL THINKING   ☐ I can justify claims I make. (p. 136)

VOCABULARY   ☐ I can use a dictionary to find the correct meanings of words. (p. 139)

GRAMMAR   ☐ I can use gerunds and infinitives as the objects of verbs. (p. 141)

PRONUNCIATION   ☐ I can put stress on important words. (p. 142)

SPEAKING   ☐ I can lead a group discussion. (p. 143)

NOTE-TAKING   ☐ I can build an outline to take notes on a discussion. (p. 145)

OBJECTIVE ▶   ☐ I can gather information and ideas to state and explain my opinions in a group discussion about research into artificial intelligence.

Economics

Can money buy happiness?

A. Discuss these questions with your classmates.

1. How much money do you think people really need in order to be happy? Explain.

2. Do you think more money would make you happier? Why or why not?

3. Look at the photo. Would you be happier if you could buy a home like this? Why or why not?

B. Listen to *The Q Classroom* online. Then answer these questions.

1. What things did the students mention they would do if they had more money?

2. According to Felix, what is something money can't buy?

iQ PRACTICE Go to the online discussion board to discuss the Unit Question with your classmates. *Practice > Unit 7 > Activity 1*

- Money - wonjob   - happy ⎰ can buy house
*   ⎱ sick - x*
Yumu - help familly   -   relationship.

Sofi - unhappy - some people.

UNIT OBJECTIVE

Listen to a presentation and an interview and gather information and ideas to participate in a group discussion evaluating the influence money has on happiness.

LISTENING 1

OBJECTIVE ▶

Sudden Wealth

You are going to listen to a presentation on how people can change when they suddenly become rich. As you listen to the presentation, gather information and ideas about money and happiness.

PREVIEW THE LISTENING

TIP FOR SUCCESS

A question and answer early in a talk often indicates the speaker's main topic.

A. PREVIEW Which topics do you think will be presented? Check (✓) your ideas.

☐ how sudden wealth makes people happy

☐ how sudden wealth causes problems

☐ the advantages and disadvantages of sudden wealth

B. VOCABULARY Read aloud these words from Listening 1. Check (✓) the ones you know. Use a dictionary to define any new or unknown words. Then discuss with a partner how the words will relate to the unit.

acquire *(v.)* 🔑 OPAL	destructive *(adj.)*	immediate *(adj.)* 🔑 OPAL
circumstances *(n.)* 🔑 OPAL	dramatic *(adj.)* 🔑	pleasure *(n.)* 🔑
complicated *(adj.)* 🔑	get used to *(phr.)*	wear off *(v. phr.)*

🔑 Oxford 3000™ words   **OPAL** Oxford Phrasal Academic Lexicon

iQ PRACTICE Go online to listen and practice your pronunciation.
Practice ▸ Unit 7 ▸ Activity 2

WORK WITH THE LISTENING

🔊 **A. LISTEN AND TAKE NOTES** Listen to the presentation about sudden wealth. Take notes in the chart as you listen.

iQ RESOURCES Go online to download extra vocabulary support.
Resources › Extra Vocabulary › Unit 7

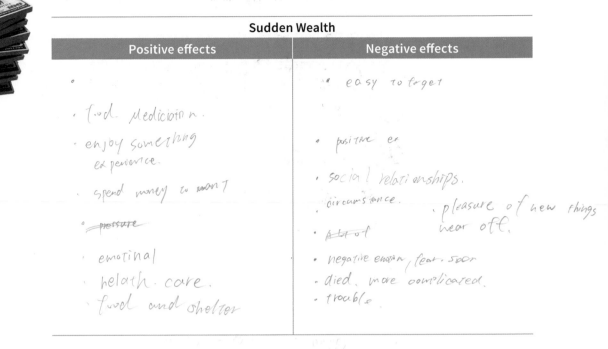

Sudden Wealth	
Positive effects	**Negative effects**

· food. medicion.
· enjoy something
  experience.
· spend money to want
· ~~pressure~~
· emotinal
· helath. care.
· food and shelter
	· easy to forget
	· positive ex
	· social relationships.
	  circumstance.
	· Alfod · pleasure of new things
	           wear off.
	· negative emotion, fear. soon
	· died. more complicated.
	· trouble

experience.
social

B. CATEGORIZE Read the statements. Write *T* (true) or *F* (false). Explain your answer with information from the listening. Then correct each false statement to make it true.

___F___ 1. Getting rich suddenly often ~~reduces~~ ^{causes} stress.

Supporting information: _People who acquire a sudden fortune . . ._
experience a lot of stress.

_T_ ___B̶___ 2. At first, acquiring a lot of money has a positive effect on our brains.

Supporting information: _____

___F___ 3. For most people, acquiring sudden wealth increases happiness.

Supporting information: _____

___T___ 4. Sudden wealth can cause many different problems.

Supporting information: _____

___T___ 5. People can feel more alone after they become suddenly wealthy.

Supporting information: _____

financial picture.

→

C. IDENTIFY Listen again. Write two examples for each main point. Compare your ideas with a partner.

[handwritten notes in left margin: immediate effect = pleasure / pleasure wears off. too many people want things from you; won't have usual sources of supports. how]

- Effect on our brains   *stress, food and medicine pressure, buy much larger*
- Effect on relationships   *understand me,*
- Effect on emotions   *fear, shein, how to get money   health care → food & shelter*

D. INTERPRET Read each situation. Based on the information in the listening, choose the best word or phrase to complete each sentence.

1. Mark got a great deal of money from his grandfather, but they didn't get along. Mark probably feels ____ .

   a. happy

   b. sad

   c. guilty *[handwritten: きいあく]*

2. Elena received a very large bonus from her job. She bought a new car. After a month, she ____ .

   a. bought a new house

   b. opened a savings account

   c. gave the money away

3. Karen received millions of dollars. She bought a house in an expensive town. After six months, she ____ .

   a. had all new friends

   b. missed her old friends

   c. felt supported in her new home

E. SYNTHESIZE Read about a Canadian couple that suddenly received a lot of money. Answer the questions according to what you learned in the listening. Discuss your answers with a partner.

Truro, Nova Scotia

Allen and Violet Large received more than $11 million in 2010. The Larges were living in Nova Scotia, Canada, and were in their 70s. Violet was getting treatment for cancer at the time. They didn't go on a spending spree. They decided to give their money away to family, charities, and even the hospital where Violet was being treated. Married for 36 years, the Larges didn't need the money. Violet said, "What you never had, you never miss." As Allen said, "We have each other."

1. How do most people respond to receiving money? How did the Larges respond differently?

2. Would the Larges be happier if they spent the money? Why or why not?

F. VOCABULARY Use the new vocabulary from Listening 1. Read the paragraphs. Then fill in each blank with the correct word or phrase from the list.

acquire (v.)	destructive (adj.)	immediate (adj.)
circumstances (n.)	dramatic (adj.)	pleasure (n.)
complicated (adj.)	get used to (phr.)	wear off (v. phr.)

A Success Story?

Thomas Carter never believed that he would _acquire_ (1) $12 million, but in 2004, that's exactly what happened. He didn't receive the money from his parents—he got it when he sold an antique vase from his attic. At the time, he only had $213 in his bank account. Tom's sudden wealth brought him a lot of _pleasure_ (2) because he could buy whatever he wanted. But this _immediate_ (3) improvement did not last long. He started to change his life in significant ways. These _dramatic_ (4) changes were hard for Tom to deal with because everything in his life became so different. Within three months, Tom had spent almost all his millions on a restaurant, a used-car lot, and an airplane. His _circumstances_ (5) had changed, but he still had trouble managing his money.

Over the next eight years, many things started happening that Tom didn't understand. His life, which had once seemed simple, was becoming more and more _complicated_ (6). The effects of his wealth soon became _destructive_ (7); it damaged many of his relationships with friends and family members. Like many people who _get used to_ (8) spending a lot of money, Tom couldn't stop even after he had lost so much of it. He continued to buy houses, cars, motorcycles, and boats. The good feeling he got from spending money started to _wear off_ (9) as time passed. Tom told people later that he was happier before he had all that money.

iQ PRACTICE Go online for more practice with the vocabulary.
Practice › Unit 7 › Activity 3

iQ PRACTICE Go online for additional listening and comprehension.
Practice › Unit 7 › Activity 4

SAY WHAT YOU THINK

DISCUSS Discuss the questions in a group.

1. Which of the effects mentioned in Listening 1 do you think are the most difficult to deal with? Why?

2. Has sudden money made anyone you know about happier or unhappier? Explain.

3. Under what circumstances do you think money could make someone happier?

LISTENING SKILL Listening for signposts

Signposts are words and phrases that can tell you the order in which things happened. Listen for signposts to help you follow the order of events and the logic in a text.

Listen to these examples of signposts from Listening 1.

First, it affects how our brains work, at least for a while.

In the beginning, when we get the money, our brain identifies it as pleasure. **Then** that feeling wears off.

Here are some words and phrases that are used as signposts.

At the start	In the middle	At the end
At first,	After (that),	Finally,
First,	Before (that),	In conclusion,
In the beginning,	Later,	In summary,
	Next,	
	Second,	
	Then,	

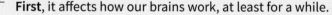

iQ RESOURCES Go online to watch the Listening Skill Video.
Resources › Video › Unit 7 › Listening Skill Video

A. IDENTIFY Listen to a reporter interview someone who suddenly acquired a lot of money. Complete the interview with the signposts you hear.

Reporter: You are one of many people in this town who suddenly acquired a lot of wealth when your company was purchased by a large software company. How has that affected your life?

Laura Green: Well, _In the beging_ , it was pretty incredible. It took a while for me to believe it. But _then_ I began to realize what it could actually do to my life. Things have changed dramatically.

Reporter: In what way?

Laura: I paid off all of my credit card debt. And sent my son to college. Receiving this money was just fantastic! _before that_ , I was worried all the time.

Reporter: So your financial circumstances have improved. What else has changed?

Laura: You know, I was a secretary at that company for 20 years. I had gotten used to just working to pay the bills. I always wished I could do more with my life. _finally_ , I can do that.

Reporter: And what do you want to do?

Laura: _first_ , I'm going to go to Paris. I've always dreamed of going there. _Next_ , I'm thinking of going back to school. I'd like to study gardening. I love flowers. _After that_ , maybe I will open my own business.

Reporter: We hear stories in the news all the time about people who get a lot of money suddenly and have many problems. How do you think those problems can be avoided?

Laura: It's about staying true to your values and remembering what's really important in life. You don't need to let money complicate things.

B. COMPOSE Answer the questions using signposts and complete sentences. Then take turns asking and answering the questions with a partner.

1. What did Laura do before she received the money?

   Before that, she worked as a secretary.

2. How did Laura feel about the money in the beginning?

   _____

3. What is one of the first things she did with the money?

   _____

4. What is Laura going to do in the immediate future?

   _____

5. What will she do next?

   _____

6. What is the last plan for the future that Laura mentions?

   _____

iQ PRACTICE Go online for more practice listening for signposts.
Practice > Unit 7 > Activity 5

LISTENING 2   # Happiness Breeds Success . . . and Money!

OBJECTIVE ▶   You are going to listen to an interview with Sonja Lyubomirsky, a psychologist who does research on happiness. As you listen to the interview, gather information and ideas about money and happiness.

Sonja Lyubomirsky

PREVIEW THE LISTENING

A. PREVIEW Which topics do you think psychologist Sonja Lyubomirsky will discuss?

- ☐ hobbies
- ☐ relationships
- ☐ travel
- ☐ income
- ☐ where people live
- ☐ work

B. VOCABULARY Read aloud these words from Listening 2. Check (✓) the ones you know. Use a dictionary to define any new or unknown words. Then discuss with a partner how the words will relate to the unit.

analysis *(n.)* 🔑 OPAL	**independence** *(n.)* OPAL
associated with *(adj. phr.)* OPAL	**outcome** *(n.)* 🔑 OPAL
burn out *(v. phr.)*	**persuasive** *(adj.)*
conduct *(v.)* 🔑 OPAL	**somewhat** *(adv.)* 🔑
demonstrate *(v.)* 🔑 OPAL	**wholly** *(adv.)*

🔑 Oxford 3000™ words   OPAL Oxford Phrasal Academic Lexicon

iQ PRACTICE Go online to listen and practice your pronunciation.
Practice > Unit 7 > Activity 7

ACADEMIC LANGUAGE
The corpus shows that *analysis* and *outcome* are common nouns in both academic writing and academic speaking.

OPAL
Oxford Phrasal Academic Lexicon

WORK WITH THE LISTENING

A. LISTEN AND TAKE NOTES Listen to the interview. Write the phrases in the correct boxes to complete the cause-effect chain.

iQ RESOURCES Go online to download extra vocabulary support.
Resources > Extra Vocabulary > Unit 7

more successful at job

- better work environment
- the happier we are
- higher income

B. IDENTIFY Listen to the interview again. Circle the best answer to the questions.

1. How did Lyubomirsky's research influence her ideas about happiness?

    a. Her research proved that our personal relationships have the greatest influence on our happiness.

    b. Although she expected relationships to influence our happiness, her research showed that work was more important.

    c. Her research showed that wealth influenced happiness more than work.

2. What qualities in a job are associated with greater happiness?

    a. productivity, creativity, and independence

    b. structure, routine, and a pleasant environment

    c. friends, a high income, and good benefits

3. What is the relationship between happiness and income?

    a. The more money we have, the happier we will be.

    b. The happier we are, the less we care about money.

    c. Happiness, job satisfaction, and income influence each other in a positive way.

C. CATEGORIZE Read the statements. Write *T* (true) or *F* (false). Then correct each false statement to make it true.

___F___ 1. Lyubomirsky and her colleagues looked at the research from 300 studies.

___T___ 2. Lyubomirsky has changed her ideas about what makes us happy.

___T___ 3. Our jobs have more of an effect on happiness than our personal relationships do.

___T___ 4. Happy people take fewer sick days than unhappy people.

___F___ 5. People who are happy when they are young will have ~~lower~~ *high* salaries when they are older.

___T___ 6. Creativity and productivity at work leads to happier workers.

D. ANALYZE Show the relationship between each pair. Use a plus sign (+) if there is a positive relationship, or a minus sign (−) if there is a negative relationship. Use Ø if there is no relationship between the two.

1. high creativity in a job   __+__ job satisfaction

2. a job that's the same every day   __−__ job satisfaction

3. higher income   __+__ happiness

4. happiness   __−__ sick days

5. happiness   __−__ burn out

6. happiness at 18   __+__ quality of job at 26

7. happiness at 18   __Ø__ size of apartment at 30

8. happiness at 21   __+__ higher income at 37

CRITICAL THINKING STRATEGY

Choosing between two or more options

To **choose** between two or more things, you need to evaluate your choices using a variety of factors, including your own knowledge and experience. Frequently when you make a choice or indicate a preference, you will have to explain *why*.

Choice	Reason (*Why?*)
I would rather have a job that paid more.	I could pay off all my bills immediately.
I prefer having a job I enjoy even if I make less money.	If I enjoy the job, I will be happier. And if I'm happier, I may do better work.

iQ PRACTICE Go online to watch the Critical Thinking Video and check your comprehension. *Practice ▶ Unit 7 ▶ Activity 6*

E. DISCUSS Discuss the questions in a group.

1. Choose which you think comes first, happiness or money. Explain.

2. What qualities of a happy person do you think lead to better employment and financial outcomes?

3. Would you choose a job that paid more money but wasn't very enjoyable, or a job that you loved but didn't pay very much? Explain.

VOCABULARY
SKILL REVIEW

In Unit 1, you learned
that suffixes help you
recognize parts of
speech. Look at the
sentences in Activity F.
Underline the common
suffixes that indicate
nouns, verbs, adjectives,
and adverbs.

F. VOCABULARY Use the new vocabulary from Listening 2. Read the sentences. Then write each bold word or phrase next to the correct definition.

1. The **analysis** of the research shows that money doesn't make people happier.

2. Sudden wealth is **associated with** stress. Many people who become rich quickly experience a lot of stress.

3. I have been working too much lately. I'm afraid I'm going to **burn out**.

4. The researchers are going to **conduct** a study on money and happiness. The study will involve 50 people.

5. Mia likes a job with **independence**. She doesn't like someone telling her what to do.

6. Researchers used the results of their study to **demonstrate** that more money does not make people happier.

7. One **outcome** of sudden wealth is a change in relationships. Others include stress and loneliness.

8. The salesman was very **persuasive**. I bought the first car he showed me!

9. I'm **somewhat** unhappy at work, but not so much that I plan to quit my job.

10. I was **wholly** to blame for the argument. You did nothing wrong.

a. _____5_____ *(n.)* the state of being free and not controlled by another person

b. _____10_____ *(adv.)* completely; fully

c. _____6_____ *(v.)* to show clearly that something exists or is true; to prove something

d. _____1_____ *(n.)* the careful examination of something

e. _____3_____ *(v. phr.)* to become very tired through overwork

f. _____4_____ *(v.)* to do, carry out, or organize something

g. _____2_____ *(adj. phr.)* connected to; involved with

h. _____7_____ *(n.)* a result or effect of an action or event

i. _____8_____ *(adj.)* able to make someone do or believe something

j. _____9_____ *(adv.)* a little

iQ PRACTICE Go online for more practice with the vocabulary.
Practice > Unit 7 > Activity 8

WORK WITH THE VIDEO

A. PREVIEW Do you think it's difficult to have a relationship with someone who has much more or much less money than you do? Why?

VIDEO VOCABULARY

estate agent (*n.*)
a person whose job is to sell houses and land for people

barista (*n.*)
a person who works in a coffee bar

reunion (*n.*)
coming together again after a separation

hippie (*n.*)
a person who rejects the way most people live, often with long hair

scruffy (*adj.*)
dirty and messy

let someone in (*v. phr.*)
allow someone to get close to you

iQ RESOURCES Go online to watch the video about two brothers.
Resources > Video > Unit 7 > Unit Video

B. CATEGORIZE Watch the video two or three times. Take notes in the first four rows of the chart.

	Ivan	David
Income level/wealth	high	low ~~builder~~
Job	politician/CEO	barista/estate agent teacher
Housing	three houses	van
Lifestyle		
Your ideas		

C. EXTEND Think about other ways that Ivan's and David's lives are different. Write your ideas in the chart. Who do you think is happier? Why?

? SAY WHAT YOU THINK

SYNTHESIZE Think about Listening 1, Listening 2, and the unit video as you discuss the questions.

1. What is the difference between sudden wealth and earning more money from a better job? Which would you prefer? Why?

2. Who do you think is more responsible for poverty—the wealthy or the poor themselves? Why do you think so?

3. How does wealth, whether you earn it, get it from family, or receive it suddenly, separate people?

VOCABULARY SKILL Idioms

Idioms are phrases that have a different meaning than the literal meanings of the individual words. Look at these examples.

☐ **Out of the blue**, Pauline found a plastic bottle.

Out of the blue means "unexpectedly." For example, storms appearing in a clear blue sky are unexpected.

☐ Communicating with a new friend from another state **is a snap** these days, thanks to the Internet and email.

To be a snap means "to be really easy." For example, making a *snapping* noise with your fingers is really easy.

Learning idioms is an important way to increase your vocabulary. English speakers use them often. As you become more familiar with idioms, you will be able to understand conversations, television programs, and radio broadcasts better.

A. IDENTIFY Work with a partner. Read the sentences. Then match each bold phrase with the correct definition on the next page.

_____ 1. I hope you have a great summer. **Drop me a line** sometime and tell me how you are doing.

_____ 2. Mark seems very upset. I think he has something he needs to **get off his chest**.

_____ 3. **Off the top of my head**, I don't have any ideas about what we should do.

_____ 4. Sometimes I can't **hold my tongue**. I always want to say what I'm feeling.

_____ 5. I'm **all ears**. How did your conversation with Professor Elliot go? I want to hear every detail!

a. listening carefully

b. without thinking first

c. to keep quiet; not to say anything

d. to talk about a problem

e. to write someone a short letter or email

TIP FOR SUCCESS

If you know all the words in a phrase, but still don't understand the meaning, the phrase might be an idiom. Idioms have to be learned by experience.

B. APPLY Complete the conversations with the idioms from Activity A. Then practice the conversations with a partner.

1. **A:** I have to do a report. Where can I find out about languages that are dying out?

   B: Hmm. I don't know ___*off the top of my head*___ , but we can look online.

2. **A:** I can't ___*hold my tongue*___ anymore. I just have to say something.

   B: That's probably not a good idea. I think you should keep quiet for a while.

3. **A:** I can't wait for my vacation. I've never been to Australia.

   B: Oh, you'll have a great time. ___*Drop me a line*___ when you can, so I know how your trip is going.

4. **A:** I have something really interesting to tell you.

   B: What is it? I'm ___*hold my tongue* all ears___ .

5. **A:** Listen, I've got something I've got to ___*get off my chest*___ . I'm really upset about it.

   B: What is it? Tell me what's wrong.

iQ PRACTICE Go online for more practice with idioms.
Practice > Unit 7 > Activity 9

SPEAKING

OBJECTIVE ▶ At the end of this unit, you will participate in a group discussion evaluating the influence money has on happiness. Make sure to use appropriate expressions for agreeing and disagreeing when you discuss this topic.

GRAMMAR Types of sentences

In English, there are four main sentence types in normal speech.

Declarative sentence (a statement):	I am trying to save money.
Interrogative sentence (a question):	How do you save money?
Imperative sentence (a direction or command):	Save your money.
Exclamatory sentence (an exclamation):	I saved so much money!

Punctuation at the end of sentences

Use periods with declarative sentences, question marks with interrogative sentences, and exclamation marks with exclamatory sentences.

Imperative sentences can end with either a period or an exclamation mark. An exclamation mark shows more emotion.

CATEGORIZE Read the conversation. Write the sentence type (declarative, interrogative, imperative, exclamatory) next to each sentence. Then practice the conversation with a partner.

_____ex_____ 1. **Hong:** There are so many cars here!

_____de_____ 2. **Nan:** Yeah, I know. It's hard to believe we can finally afford a new one.

_____de_____ 3. **Hong:** I'm just glad we got the money as a reward for helping someone.

_____de_____ 4. **Nan:** Me too. I didn't even know your uncle very well.

_____inte_____ 5. **Hong:** Didn't you meet him at the wedding?

_____de_____ 6. **Nan:** Yes, but I only had a short conversation with him.

_____de_____ 7. **Hong:** I had no idea that he was going to give us so much money.

_____impe_____ 8. **Nan:** Speaking of money, hold my purse for a minute. I can't find my wallet!

iQ PRACTICE Go online for more practice with sentence types.
Practice ▶ Unit 7 ▶ Activity 10

166 UNIT 7 Can money buy happiness?

iQ PRACTICE   Go online for the Grammar Expansion: word order in different types of sentences. *Practice › Unit 7 › Activity 11*

PRONUNCIATION Intonation in different types of sentences

Intonation varies according to **sentence type**. Learning intonation patterns can help you understand if a speaker is asking a question, giving a command, or making a statement.

Declarative and imperative sentences:

Declarative and imperative sentences have a falling intonation.

I am going to purchase a new home.

Please give me some advice.

Exclamatory sentences:

Exclamatory sentences have a rise-fall intonation.

This is fun!

Interrogative sentences:

Remember that interrogative sentences or questions have two intonation patterns. *Yes/no* questions have a rising intonation pattern.

Are you coming with me?

Wh- questions have a falling intonation pattern.

Why did you leave?

A. IDENTIFY Listen to the sentences. Check (✓) the type of sentence for each according to the intonation you hear.

1. a. ☐ statement   ☑ *yes/no* question
   b. ☑ statement   ☐ *yes/no* question
2. a. ☑ command   ☐ *wh-* question
   b. ☐ command   ☑ *wh-* question
3. a. ☑ statement   ☐ exclamation
   b. ☐ statement   ☑ exclamation

B. APPLY Listen again. Repeat the sentences using the same intonation that you hear.

iQ PRACTICE   Go online for more practice with intonation in different types of sentences. *Practice › Unit 7 › Activity 12*

We can use certain phrases for **agreeing** and **disagreeing**. It's important to know which phrases and expressions are appropriate for formal and informal situations. An informal conversation is very different from a formal discussion at college or at work.

Here are some expressions you can use when you want to agree or disagree in different situations.

Agreeing		Disagreeing
I agree (completely).	formal	I disagree.
That's exactly what I think.		I don't agree (at all).
That's a good point.		Sorry, but that's not my opinion.
That's right.		I don't feel the same way.
I think so too.		I don't think so.
Absolutely!		No way!
Yeah, I know!	informal	Oh, come on!

IDENTIFY Listen to the conversations. Complete each conversation with the expressions you hear.

1. **Ellie:** What are you going to do with the money your grandfather gave you?

   Sam: I'm not sure. I think I'm going to take an expensive vacation.

   Ellie: Really? Don't you have a lot of school loans to pay?

   Sam: _That's a good point_ . Maybe the vacation's not such a good idea.

1

   Ellie: _You can say that again_ ! Vacations are fun, but it's much more

2
   important to pay off your debt.

2. **Monica:** I think raising the average income in countries around the world is the best way to increase the level of happiness.

   Patricia: I _don't feel the same way_. More money might make the very

3
   poor happier, but not everyone.

   Monica: I _disagree !_ . I think everyone except perhaps the

4
   very wealthy will benefit from a higher income.

   Patricia: Well, I can see we'll just have to agree to disagree.

   iQ PRACTICE Go online for more practice with agreeing and disagreeing.
   Practice › Unit 7 › Activity 13

NOTE-TAKING SKILL Taking and organizing notes from a discussion

Sometimes it is important to take notes from a pair or group discussion. You may need to report on the discussion to the class, or you may want to use the ideas from the discussion to prepare for a test, write an essay, or make a presentation. One way to organize your notes is by using a graphic organizer. For a pair discussion, you can use a Venn diagram. This allows you to show points of agreement and disagreement.

 A. INVESTIGATE Listen to an excerpt from a discussion about happiness. Then take notes in the Venn diagram. Compare your notes with a partner.

First speaker's ideas   Both speakers agree   Second speaker's ideas

- pay on my bill
- bill need house
- stay nice hotel

- and car experience
- stay

- h
- relax
- rich → happen
- just need enjoy
- camp - hostel stay
- experience

B. INTERPRET Use your notes to answer the questions.

1. What is the topic of the discussion?

2. What information do they give to support their ideas?

3. What do the two speakers agree about?

4. What do they disagree about?

C. RESTATE With a partner, summarize the speakers' points using the notes from the graphic organizer.

iQ PRACTICE Go online for more practice taking and organizing notes from a discussion. *Practice > Unit 7 > Activity 14*

Chiang Mai, Thailand

UNIT ASSIGNMENT   Take part in a group discussion

OBJECTIVE ▶

In this assignment, you are going to take part in a group discussion about money and happiness. As you prepare for the discussion, think about the Unit Question, "Can money buy happiness?" Use information from Listening 1, Listening 2, the unit video, and your work in this unit to support your discussion. Refer to the Self-Assessment checklist on page 172.

CONSIDER THE IDEAS

DISCUSS Work with a partner. Discuss the questions about money and happiness. Be sure to use the correct intonation when you ask each other questions.

What is money's influence on happiness?

What kind of person do you think would be happier with more money? Why?

Would your life be different if you had more or less money? How?

Is it more enjoyable to give or receive money? Why?

PREPARE AND SPEAK

TIP FOR SUCCESS

When disagreeing with someone, you can sound more polite by starting with *I know what you mean, but . . .* or *I see your point, but . . .*

A. **GATHER IDEAS** Take notes on your discussion with your partner. Use these questions to guide you.

1. What were the main points of your discussion?

2. What did you agree on?

3. What did you disagree on?

B. **ORGANIZE IDEAS** Choose one question from the Consider the Ideas activity. Use the outline to help you prepare for a group discussion. Do not write exactly what you are going to say. Just write notes to help you organize your ideas.

Question: _____

Ideas that I agree with: _____

_____

_____

Ideas that I disagree with: _____

_____

_____

My answer to the question: _____

_____

_____

Reasons for my answer: _____

_____

_____

Examples: _____

_____

_____

C. **SPEAK** Work in a group. Take turns presenting your ideas on the questions you chose in Activity B. Refer to the Self-Assessment checklist on page 172 before you begin.

iQ PRACTICE   Go online for your alternate Unit Assignment.
Practice > *Unit 7* > *Activity 15*

CHECK AND REFLECT

A. CHECK Think about the Unit Assignment as you complete the Self-Assessment checklist.

SELF-ASSESSMENT	Yes	No
I was able to speak easily about the topic.	☐	☐
My group understood me.	☐	☐
I used vocabulary from the unit.	☐	☐
I used different types of sentences when speaking.	☐	☐
I used different intonation patterns.	☐	☐
I used expressions for agreeing and disagreeing.	☐	☐

B. REFLECT Discuss these questions with a partner or group.

1. What is something new you learned in this unit?

2. Look back at the Unit Question—Can money buy happiness? Is your answer different now than when you started this unit? If yes, how is it different? Why?

iQ PRACTICE Go to the online discussion board to discuss the questions.
Practice > Unit 7 > Activity 16

TRACK YOUR SUCCESS

iQ PRACTICE Go online to check the words and phrases you have learned in this unit. *Practice > Unit 7 > Activity 17*

Check (✓) the skills you learned. If you need more work on a skill, refer to the page(s) in parentheses.

LISTENING ☐ I can listen for signposts. (p. 156)

CRITICAL THINKING ☐ I can choose between two or more options using experience and knowledge. (p. 161)

VOCABULARY ☐ I can use idioms. (p. 164)

GRAMMAR ☐ I can use different types of sentences. (p. 166)

PRONUNCIATION ☐ I can use correct intonation in different types of sentences. (p. 167)

SPEAKING ☐ I can use expressions for agreeing and disagreeing. (p. 168)

NOTE-TAKING ☐ I can take and organize notes from a discussion. (p. 169)

OBJECTIVE ▶ ☐ I can gather information and ideas to participate in a group discussion evaluating the influence money has on happiness.

8 Behavioral Science

What can we learn from success and failure?

A. Discuss these questions with your classmates.

1. What are some of the different ways a person can be successful?

2. In what ways do you think you are successful?

3. Look at the photo. What is happening? In what ways has this person been successful?

B. Listen to *The Q Classroom* online. Then answer these questions.

1. What types of success do the students mention? Do you agree or disagree with their ideas? Why?

2. How important does Marcus think failures are? How does he explain his opinion?

iQ PRACTICE   Go to the online discussion board to discuss the Unit Question with your classmates. *Practice > Unit 8 > Activity 1*

UNIT OBJECTIVE

Listen to a panel discussion and an interview and gather information and ideas to discuss successful and unsuccessful personal experiences and explain what you learned from them.

LISTENING 1

OBJECTIVE ▶

Learning from Failure

You are going to listen to a panel discussion between several experts. As you listen, gather information and ideas about what we can learn from success and failure.

PREVIEW THE LISTENING

A. PREVIEW Which things do you think the experts will say are lessons to be learned from failure? Check (✓) your answers.

- ☑ Don't give up.
- ☐ Don't focus on rejection.
- ☐ If one thing can't work, move on to something else.
- ☐ Don't trust other people.
- ☑ Discover your real strengths.
- ☐ No one truly fails.

ACADEMIC LANGUAGE
The corpus shows that *failure* is a common noun in both academic speaking and academic writing.

_____ OPAL
Oxford Phrasal Academic Lexicon

B. VOCABULARY Read aloud these words from Listening 1. Check (✓) the ones you know. Use a dictionary to define any new or unknown words. Then discuss with a partner how the words will relate to the unit.

all along *(adv. phr.)*	**give up** *(v. phr.)*	**material** *(n.)* 🔑 OPAL
blame *(v.)* 🔑	**go into** *(v. phr.)*	**painful** *(adj.)* 🔑
bring up *(v. phr.)*	**highlight** *(v.)* 🔑 OPAL	**sincere** *(adj.)* 🔑
failure *(n.)* 🔑 OPAL		

🔑 Oxford 3000™ words   **OPAL** Oxford Phrasal Academic Lexicon

iQ PRACTICE Go online to listen and practice your pronunciation.
Practice > Unit 8 > Activity 2

J. K. Rowling   Ang Lee   Thomas Edison

WORK WITH THE LISTENING

🔊 **A. LISTEN AND TAKE NOTES** Listen to the panel discussion. Complete the chart with the missing words.

iQ RESOURCES Go online to download extra vocabulary support.
Resources > Extra Vocabulary > Unit 8

Main Points	Examples
1. J. K. Rowling experienced failure before her books about ~~Harry Potter~~ became a success.	• was unemployed • was ~~poor~~ • book samples rejected
2. Ang Lee has used ~~failure~~ as a sign of what to do next.	• art school instead of university • switched to ~~work directing~~ instead of acting
3. Thomas Edison repeatedly tried new ~~materials~~ for making his light bulb.	• tried 6,000 types of ~~plant~~ material

B. EVALUATE The panel members use stories to make their points. Do you think this is an effective technique? Why or why not?

🔊 **C. IDENTIFY** Listen to the panel discussion again. Circle the answer that best completes each statement according to what the speakers say.

1. Just before getting a publisher for *Harry Potter*, J. K. Rowling did not have a
   _____.

   a. home   b. job

2. In the "Fishing Syndrome," a creative person has not found _____ piece of their creative work.

   a. anyone who will accept a   b. an idea that will make a good

3. Ang Lee became a director because his _____ skills were weak.

   a. acting   b. English

4. Thomas Edison's search for a long-lasting light bulb took a long time because he had to _____.

   a. do all the work by himself   b. try thousands of materials

5. Edison wanted people to know he was working on light bulbs because he wanted _____ from the public.

   a. attention   b. suggestions

D. CATEGORIZE Read the statements. Write *T* (true) or *F* (false). Then correct each false statement to make it true.

____ 1. J. K. Rowling has earned more than $1 billion from her writing.

____ 2. The male expert on the panel says that the main lesson from Rowling's experience is, "Keep trying."

____ 3. Ang Lee's films are famous in his home country, but he has not yet succeeded internationally.

____ 4. The female expert on the panel says that Lee uses failure as an indication of which direction to take.

____ 5. Thomas Edison invented the first working electric light bulb.

____ 6. The male expert believes Edison truly meant his statements about failure.

VOCABULARY SKILL REVIEW

Remember to read the whole sentence and consider the *context*. This can help you identify the correct word and meaning.

E. VOCABULARY Use the new vocabulary from Listening 1. Read the sentences. Circle the answer that best matches the meaning of each bold word or phrase.

1. The climb was difficult, but **all along,** I knew that reaching the mountaintop was worth it.

   a. for everyone   b. the whole time   c. at the hardest times

2. The boy broke a dish and then tried to **blame** his brother for it.

   a. accuse   b. thank   c. hurt

3. My friend was in a bad car accident as a child, so I don't **bring up** accidents to her.

   a. laugh about   b. cause   c. mention

4. Losing the soccer tournament was **painful**, but the players knew they had tried their best.

   a. upsetting   b. easy   c. boring

5. Her first attempt to become the mayor of her town ended in **failure**, but she succeeded two years later.

   a. a good lesson   b. disaster   c. lack of success

6. I expected the tired runner to **give up**, but she finished the race.

   a. decide to stop   b. let someone else win   c. need medical care

7. Even as a child, he was interested in rocks. I'm not surprised he wants to **go into** geology.

   a. talk about   b. start a career in   c. travel to

8. There are many reasons to eat fruit, but let me just **highlight** your body's need for vitamin C.

   a. do some research on   b. speak quickly about   c. pay special attention to

9. Which **material** is better for food containers—glass or plastic?

   a. content   b. style   c. substance

10. Unfortunately, politicians often say things you want to hear, but they're not always **sincere** about them.

    a. clear   b. honest   c. happy

iQ PRACTICE Go online for more practice with the vocabulary.
Practice > Unit 8 > Activity 3

iQ PRACTICE Go online for additional listening and comprehension.
Practice > Unit 8 > Activity 4

SAY WHAT YOU THINK

DISCUSS Discuss the questions in a group.

1. Do you agree that the experiences of successful people can teach us about failure? Why or why not?

2. Think of someone you know who has experienced failure but has succeeded anyway. What do you think he or she learned from failure?

3. Is failure always a positive learning experience? Explain.

Listening for **examples** will help you understand a speaker's main points more clearly. Speakers often introduce examples with a common phrase that tells you that an example follows.

For example,	such as	To give (you) an example,
For instance,	Take, for example,	To illustrate this,

 A. IDENTIFY Listen to the panel discussion again. Make a list of the phrases the speakers use to signal examples.

 B. IDENTIFY Listen to Paul talk about how his view of failure has changed. List each example he gives. You do not need to write full sentences.

1. Paul says that when he was in high school, he used to "lead all sorts of activities." ~expect~ ~president school~

   Example: _____

2. He says that after he lost the election, he felt that his "self-confidence was destroyed." ~everyone look at him like looser~

   Example: _____ ~and think he is~

3. Paul says he learned "some things about leadership" from losing the election.
   ~not ready to government~
   Example: _____ ~college~ _____

4. He also says that it was good for him to "just be a normal student."
   ~time to make friend enjoy some event~
   Example: _____

C. EXTEND Think about a time when you learned some lessons by failing at something. Briefly describe two or three lessons you learned.

What you failed at: _____

Lessons you learned: _____

_____

_____

_____

_____

D. DISCUSS Work with a partner. Take turns talking about your failures and the lessons you learned. Use phrases from the Listening Skill box on page 180 when you give examples. Take notes below as you listen to your partner.

What your partner failed at: _____

Lessons your partner learned:_____

_____

_____

_____

_____

iQ PRACTICE   Go online for more practice listening for examples.
Practice ⟩ Unit 8 ⟩ Activity 5

CRITICAL THINKING STRATEGY

Paraphrasing

When you **paraphrase** a statement by someone else, you express the same meaning in your own words. A paraphrase, unlike a summary, is about as long as the original statement. It also has the same basic meaning as the original, but the wording, grammar, and maybe even the order of ideas are your own. A good paraphrase shows that you understood the original idea.

Original	Paraphrase
A positive view of failure keeps a person from unproductive and time-wasting rounds of fretting and self-blame.	If you see failure as a good thing, you won't waste time in uselessly worrying about things and blaming yourself.
No one has ever succeeded entirely by his own efforts, without aid from others.	Every successful person has had help from other people.
Sometimes, people want so badly to succeed that they try too hard and make errors that could have been avoided.	*Compose your own paraphrase:*

iQ PRACTICE   Go online to watch the Critical Thinking Video and check your comprehension. *Practice ⟩ Unit 8 ⟩ Activity 6*

E. APPLY Look back at your notes about the lessons your partner learned from failure. Paraphrase his or her failures and lessons for the class.

An Interview with Mohannad Abu-dayyah

OBJECTIVE ▶

You are going to listen to an interview with Mohannad Abu-dayyah, a well-known inventor from Saudi Arabia. As you listen to the interview, gather information and ideas about what we can learn from success and failure.

PREVIEW THE LISTENING

Mohannad Abu-dayyah has found success as an inventor despite losing his eyesight and one leg in an accident at the age of 20. He went on to establish the Isterlab Training Center, where he leads and manages projects on innovation. Mohannad is now an internationally recognized figure in the field of invention and innovation.

Mohannad Abu-dayyah

A. PREVIEW What challenges do you think Mohannad has had to overcome in order to be successful? What does his success tell you about his character? Make a list of your ideas, and then compare with a partner.

B. VOCABULARY Read aloud these words from Listening 2. Check (✓) the ones you know. Use a dictionary to define any new or unknown words. Then discuss with a partner how the words will relate to the unit.

award (n.) 🔑	**disability** (n.)	**supportive** (adj.)
blind (adj.) 🔑	**incredibly** (adv.) 🔑	**tricky** (adj.)
convincing (adj.)	**innovate** (v.)	
crash (n.) 🔑	**inspiration** (n.)	

🔑 Oxford 3000™ words

iQ PRACTICE   Go online to listen and practice your pronunciation.
Practice > Unit 8 > Activity 7

WORK WITH THE LISTENING

A. LISTEN AND TAKE NOTES   Go online to listen to the first part of the interview and take notes in the chart.

iQ RESOURCES   Go online to download extra vocabulary support.
Resources > Extra Vocabulary > Unit 8

	Challenges
1. Before his accident	
2. After his accident	

B. IDENTIFY   Circle the answer that best completes each statement.

1. Mohannad's disabilities are the result of _____ accident.

   a. a flying

   b. an industrial

   c. a traffic

2. At the time of the accident he was _____.

   a. studying at a university

   b. employed in a factory

   c. planning his wedding

3. He has a degree in _____.

   a. invention

   b. design

   c. engineering

4. He started inventing when he was _____.

   a. a college student

   b. a young child

   c. a teenager

5. He believes the key to his success is _____.

   a. good fortune

   b. intelligence

   c. determination

C. CATEGORIZE Read the statements. Listen to the rest of the interview. Write *T* (true) or *F* (false). Then correct each false statement to make it true.

  T 1. Mohannad has invented many things to help people with disabilities.

  F 2. He first won an award for invention at the age of 14.

  T 3. He was inspired by watching programs about famous successful people.

  F 4. He sees failure as an enemy.

  F 5. Today, his view of success is the same as when he was a child.

D. IDENTIFY Listen again and complete the sentences.

1. Mohannad received an award from __King Abdulla__ for inventing a submarine.

2. He has written a book called _____guidance_____ for Leading Invention.

3. He is grateful to his _____wife_____, family, and friends for their support.

4. More than ___30,000___ people have taken part in courses given by the Isterlab Training Center.

5. He hopes to inspire ___1 million___ inventors across the Arab world.

E. EVALUATE With a partner, discuss how Mohannad's view of success has changed over time. Then look at the list below. Which of these factors apply to Mohannad? Which do you think are the most important?

hard work   interest from an early age

supportive friends and family   self-belief

appropriate qualifications   determination

F. DISCUSS Discuss the questions in a group.

1. Mohannad says, "I see failure as a friend who teaches you to become successful." To what extent do you agree?

2. Give an example of a time when you succeeded after failing at first. What did you learn from your mistakes?

G. VOCABULARY Use the new vocabulary from Listening 2. Circle the answer that best matches the meaning of each bold word.

TIP FOR SUCCESS

Making lists of words with similar meanings, or *synonyms*, is a good way to expand your vocabulary. Use a dictionary to study differences in meaning.

1. **award** *(n.)*	gift	excellence	prize
2. **blind** *(adj.)*	sightless	apart	invisible
3. **convincing** *(adj.)*	debating	worthwhile	appealing
4. **crash** *(n.)*	break	noise	collision
5. **disability** *(n.)*	incapacity	unusual	attempt
6. **incredibly** *(adv.)*	supreme	rely	unbelievably
7. **innovate** *(v.)*	invent	relation	fortune
8. **inspiration** *(n.)*	confidence	motivation	succeed
9. **supportive** *(adj.)*	weight	helpful	accessory
10. **tricky** *(adj.)*	deceive	unused	problematic

iQ PRACTICE Go online for more practice with the vocabulary.
Practice > Unit 8 > Activity 8

WORK WITH THE VIDEO

VIDEO VOCABULARY

futile (*adj.*) (used about an action) having no effect or result; useless

surge (*n.*) a sudden increase in something

inland (*adj.*) in an area that is far from the coast

devastation (*n.*) complete destruction

A. PREVIEW You will watch a video about damage that occurred after a system of protective structures failed because of a hurricane. Before you watch, consider the questions:

1. Which aspects of a strong hurricane can damage cities?

2. What can communities do to prepare for a strong hurricane?

iQ RESOURCES Go online to watch the video about Hurricane Katrina.
Resources > Video > Unit 8 > Unit Video

B. IDENTIFY Watch the video two or three times. Circle the correct answers to the questions.

1. What specific event related to Hurricane Katrina caused the city's system of levees (flood walls) to fail?

   a. strong winds   b. high water levels   c. changing tides

2. Why were the levees not good enough?

   a. too tall   b. too weak   c. too new

3. According to Dr. Van Heerden, what conditions might make it necessary to abandon cities like New Orleans?

   a. people leaving   b. damage from Katrina   c. higher sea levels

C. EXTEND What lessons do you think we can learn from the failures that occurred around New Orleans as a result of Hurricane Katrina? Discuss with a partner. Then share your ideas with the class.

SAY WHAT YOU THINK

SYNTHESIZE Think about the unit video, Listening 1, and Listening 2 as you discuss the questions.

1. How does Mohannad's experience support what the panelists said in Listening 1?

2. In what ways, if any, has your view of success and failure changed?

VOCABULARY SKILL Prefixes

Prefixes are added to the beginning of words to change their meaning. Understanding prefixes can help you expand your vocabulary and figure out the meaning of unknown words.

Notice the use of prefixes in these examples from Listening 2.

- I liked to **re**design my toys.
- People thought it was **im**possible to dive so deep.

Many prefixes give the opposite meaning to words.

- **dis-** **dis**agree
- **im-** (before words beginning with *m* or *p*) **im**mature, **im**polite
- **ir-** (before words beginning with *r*) **ir**rational

These prefixes give other meanings to words.

- **co-** (together) **co**operate   **multi-** (many) **multi**purpose
- **re-** (again) **re**place, **re**write   **anti-** (against) **anti**war

A. COMPOSE Add a prefix from the Vocabulary Skill box to complete each word.

1. __*re*__ view
2. _____ responsible
3. _____ like
4. _____ worker
5. _____ perfect
6. _____ social
7. _____ national
8. _____ honest
9. _____ patient
10. _____ regular
11. _____ apply
12. _____ media

B. CREATE Choose three words from Activity A. Write a sentence using each word.

C. IDENTIFY Read your sentences to a partner. Take notes on any words you hear from Activity A. Underline the prefixes.

iQ PRACTICE Go online for more practice with prefixes.
Practice > Unit 8 > Activity 9

SPEAKING

At the end of this unit, you will take part in a discussion about success and failure. Make sure to ask for and give clarification when you discuss the topic.

GRAMMAR Simple past and present perfect

Use the **simple past** for actions that began and ended in the past. For actions that began in the past and continue up to the present, use the **present perfect**.

Simple past

Mohannad Abu-dayyah **studied** industrial engineering at King Fahd University.
(He no longer studies industrial engineering. He finished his degree.)

Present perfect

Mohannad **has given** many presentations on innovation.
(He is still giving presentations on innovation.)

Use the simple past for actions that occurred at a specific time in the past. If the time an action occurred is not known or not important, use the present perfect.

Simple past

Mohannad **won** his first award at the age of 12.

Present perfect

Mohannad **has won** many awards.
(The exact dates he won the awards are not important.)

Use the present perfect for actions that happened more than once in the past when the focus is on how often the actions happened rather than when they happened.

Mohannad fails sometimes. He **has learned** from his mistakes.

Time expressions used with the simple past and present perfect

Last, ago, in, and *on* are commonly used with the simple past to show that an action was completed in the past.

For and *since* are commonly used with the present perfect to show that an action is connected to the present.

Mohannad founded the Isterlab Training Center **eight years ago**.
He has worked there **for eight years**.

iQ RESOURCES Go online to watch the Grammar Skill Video.
Resources › Video › Unit 8 › Grammar Skill Video

A. IDENTIFY Circle the correct verb forms to complete the conversation. Then practice the conversation with a partner.

Ashley: Hey, Kevin. Great shot! You know, you're a pretty good tennis player. (Did you ever enter / ~~Have you ever entered~~) any tennis competitions?
1

Kevin: Yes, I (did / ~~have~~). Actually, I (~~came~~ / have come) in second in the
2   3
Senior Tournament at our club last year.

Ashley: Really? That's great. (Did you enjoy / Have you enjoyed) it?
4

Kevin: Sure! Especially because it (was / ~~has been~~) my first attempt. How about
5
you?

Ashley: Oh, I play in a small local league, but I (~~didn't win~~ / haven't won) any
6
competitions or anything. I just play for fun, to keep fit and healthy.

B. CREATE Think of a hobby or sport that you enjoy. Note your answers to these questions. Then ask and answer the questions with a partner.

1. What hobby or sport do you enjoy? _I enjoy badminton._

2. How long have you done it? _I have done it for 3 years._

3. Why do you like it? _Because I can only play badminton._

4. Have you ever entered any competitions? _No_

5. In what ways are you "successful" at your hobby or sport?
   Continue playing it from my whole

C. EXTEND Complete each statement with your own ideas. Then compare sentences with a partner.

1. I _____ lately.

2. I _____ since last week.

3. I _____ yet.

4. I _____ a few years ago.

5. I _____ yesterday.

iQ PRACTICE Go online for more practice with the simple past and present perfect. *Practice* > *Unit 8* > *Activity 10*

iQ PRACTICE Go online for the Grammar Expansion: present perfect continuous. *Practice* > *Unit 8* > *Activity 11*

PRONUNCIATION Varying intonation to maintain interest

You can help your listeners follow what you are saying more easily, and also help to keep them interested while you are speaking, by varying your intonation—making your voice rise and fall—a little more than usual.

Listen to this sentence from the interview with Mohannad. You will hear it twice. Notice how the speaker sounds more interested the second time, and this makes it more interesting and easier to follow.

 ☐ I see failure as a friend who teaches you how to become successful.

Listen to some more examples. Notice how the speaker varies her intonation to make what she says sound more interesting and easier to follow.

 You can learn more from your failures than you can from your successes.

Success for my grandfather is getting out of bed in the morning!

Failing is a good preparation for life.

 A. IDENTIFY Listen twice to each sentence. Who sounds more interested, Speaker 1 or Speaker 2?

	Speaker 1	Speaker 2
1. Failure is an important stage on the road to success.	☐	☐
2. We shouldn't be afraid of failure because we can learn from it.	☐	☐
3. Failure is something to be encouraged by.	☐	☐
4. Don't give up too easily.	☐	☐

B. APPLY Listen again. Repeat the sentences, using the same intonation you hear.

C. APPLY Read the paragraph below. Think about how you can use intonation to make it sound interesting and easier for listeners to follow. With a partner, take turns reading the paragraph aloud.

You need to experience failure and learn from it, in order to really succeed. Failing is a good preparation for life. It makes you stronger and more able to overcome life's problems. Don't be scared of failure! It might sound strange, but letting go of your fear of failure might help you to succeed.

D. IDENTIFY Listen and check your answers to Activity C. Then listen and repeat, using the same intonation.

 iQ PRACTICE Go online for more practice varying intonation to maintain interest. *Practice > Unit 8 > Activity 12*

After you listen to a speech or presentation, you can ask questions if you need **clarification** or more information about something the speaker said. Asking questions shows that you are interested and have been paying attention.

Asking for clarification

Sorry, I don't get what you mean.

What do you mean exactly?

Could you say a bit more about . . . ?

Can you give an example?

After giving a speech or presentation, it is a good idea to ask the audience for questions. This gives you an opportunity to clarify your most important points and make sure your audience understood them.

Giving clarification

What I'm trying to say . . .

To give you an example . . .

I mean . . .

 A. IDENTIFY Listen to the excerpts from a discussion. Complete the excerpts wth the phrases you hear. Then practice the conversations with a partner.

1. **Professor:** So you need to make sure the success you're aiming for is achievable.

   Student 1: _____ .
   ₁

   Professor: What _____ , be realistic with the goals
   ₂
   you set for yourself.

2. **Professor:** Success in one area can bring problems in others.

   Student 2: _____ ?
   ₃

   Professor: Well, _____ , someone can be at the top
   ₄
   of her career, but her family life might be in crisis as a result.

3. **Professor:** Keep your desire for success in proportion.

   Student 3: _____ ?
   ₅

   Professor: Yes. I mean don't let your desire for success become greater than other important areas in your life.

4. **Professor:** Our definition of success alters with age.

   Student 1: _____?
   ₆

   Professor: Sure. Someone of 20 might view success as being rich, but at 50 that same person might think of success as a happy family life.

B. APPLY Work with a partner. Take turns reading the statements aloud and asking for and giving clarification.

1. Failure is an important stage on the road to success.

   A: Sorry, I don't get what you mean.

   B: What I mean by that is we learn from our mistakes.

2. If at first you don't succeed, try, try again.

3. Success for my grandfather is simply getting out of bed in the morning.

4. Failing is a good preparation for life.

iQ PRACTICE Go online for more practice asking for and giving clarification.
Practice > Unit 8 > Activity 13

NOTE-TAKING SKILL Taking notes with examples

When discussing a topic, you may want to give examples to help support your opinion. Taking notes with examples is therefore a very useful skill. It allows you to organize your ideas and support your opinions in a way that is easy to refer to when you are speaking.

Look at these main points and examples from Listening 1. Notice how the main points are noted separately, next to the supporting examples.

Main points	Examples
1. We cannot avoid failure.	Rowling: It's impossible to live without failing at something
2. Don't blame yourself.	Fishing syndrome Thinking no one wants what you've created
3. Don't let failure blind you.	• Rowling's work was fine, she kept going. • Ang changed his plans • Edison tried more materials

CREATE Think of different examples to support each main point in the chart below. Then discuss the topic of success with a partner.

Main points	Examples
1. We cannot avoid failure.	
2. Don't blame yourself.	
3. Don't let failure blind you.	

iQ PRACTICE Go online for more practice taking notes with examples.
Practice > Unit 8 > Activity 14

UNIT ASSIGNMENT Take part in a pair discussion

OBJECTIVE ▶

In this assignment, you are going to take part in a discussion about success and failure. As you prepare for the discussion, think about the Unit Question, "What can we learn from success and failure?" Use information from Listening 1, Listening 2, the unit video, and your work in this unit to support your discussion. Refer to the Self-Assessment checklist on page 196.

CONSIDER THE IDEAS

INTERPRET Work with a partner. Read the quotes about success and failure. Decide what each quote means, and think of an example for it. Take notes in the charts. Then explain to your partner whether you agree or disagree with the quote.

> "Success is not the key to happiness. Happiness is the key to success. If you love what you are doing, you will be successful."
>
> —*Albert Schweitzer*

Meaning	Example

> "Success is never final. Failure is never fatal. Courage is what counts."
>
> —*Winston Churchill*

Meaning	Example

> "Many of life's failures are people who did not realize how close they were to success when they gave up."
>
> —*Thomas Edison*

Meaning	Example

PREPARE AND SPEAK

A. GATHER IDEAS Think about what success means to you. Complete the activities.

1. Make a list of things you have been successful at. They can be big things, such as graduating from high school, or small things, such as cooking a delicious meal.

2. Now make a list of things you have tried but were not successful at. Again, they can be big things, such as applying for a job, or small things, such as playing a game of tennis.

B. ORGANIZE IDEAS Choose one example from each list in Activity A. Complete the outline to help you prepare to discuss your ideas.

1. Something I was successful at: _____

What difficulties did you experience?

_____

_____

How has this experience affected your life?

_____

_____

What have you learned from this experience?

_____

_____

2. Something I was unsuccessful at: _____

What difficulties did you experience?

_____

_____

How has this experience affected your life?

_____

_____

What have you learned from this experience?

_____

_____

C. SPEAK Complete these steps. Refer to the Self-Assessment checklist below before you begin.

1. Work with a partner. Take turns telling each other about your experiences.

2. Discuss which experience you learned more from. Do not read directly from your outline. Just use it to help you remember your ideas. Use phrases from the Speaking Skill box on page 191 to ask for and give clarification.

iQ PRACTICE   Go online for your alternate Unit Assignment.
Practice > Unit 8 > Activity 15

CHECK AND REFLECT

A. CHECK Think about the Unit Assignment as you complete the Self-Assessment checklist.

SELF-ASSESSMENT	Yes	No
I was able to speak easily about the topic.	☐	☐
My partner understood me.	☐	☐
I used vocabulary from the unit.	☐	☐
I used the simple past and present perfect.	☐	☐
I varied my intonation to maintain interest.	☐	☐
I asked for and gave clarification.	☐	☐
I paraphrased statements by others.	☐	☐

B. REFLECT Discuss these questions with a partner or group.

1. What is something new you learned in this unit?

2. Look back at the Unit Question—What can we learn from success and failure? Is your answer different now than when you started this unit? If yes, how is it different? Why?

iQ PRACTICE   Go to the online discussion board to discuss the questions.
Practice > Unit 8 > Activity 16

TRACK YOUR SUCCESS

iQ PRACTICE Go online to check the words and phrases you have learned in this unit. *Practice > Unit 8 > Activity 17*

Check (✓) the skills you learned. If you need more work on a skill, refer to the page(s) in parentheses.

LISTENING	☐ I can listen for examples. (p. 180)
CRITICAL THINKING	☐ I can paraphrase statements. (p.181)
VOCABULARY	☐ I can use prefixes. (p. 187)
GRAMMAR	☐ I can use the simple past and present perfect. (p. 188)
PRONUNCIATION	☐ I can vary intonation to maintain interest. (p. 190)
SPEAKING	☐ I can ask for and give clarification. (p. 191)
NOTE-TAKING	☐ I can take notes with examples. (p. 193)

OBJECTIVE ▶ ☐ I can gather information and ideas to discuss successful and unsuccessful personal experiences and explain what I learned from them.

VOCABULARY LIST AND CEFR CORRELATION

🔑 The **Oxford 3000™** is a list of the 3,000 core words that every learner of English needs to know. The words have been chosen based on their frequency in the Oxford English Corpus and relevance to learners of English. Every word is aligned to the CEFR, guiding learners on the words they should know at the A1–B2 level.

OPAL The **Oxford Phrasal Academic Lexicon** is an essential guide to the most important words and phrases to know for academic English. The word lists are based on the Oxford Corpus of Academic English and the British Academic Spoken English corpus.

The **Common European Framework of Reference for Language (CEFR)** provides a basic description of what language learners have to do to use language effectively. The system contains 6 reference levels: A1, A2, B1, B2, C1, C2.

UNIT 1

assess *(v.)* 🔑 OPAL B2
association *(n.)* 🔑 OPAL B2
assume *(v.)* 🔑 OPAL B2
behavior *(n.)* OPAL A2
briefly *(adv.)* OPAL B2
concentrate *(v.)* 🔑 OPAL B1
conscious *(adj.)* 🔑 B2
effective *(adj.)* 🔑 OPAL B1
encounter *(n.)* OPAL B2
error *(n.)* 🔑 OPAL A2
expert *(n.)* 🔑 OPAL A2
familiar *(adj.)* 🔑 OPAL B1
form an impression *(v. phr.)* B1
negative *(adj.)* 🔑 OPAL A1
observation *(n.)* 🔑 OPAL B2
positive *(adj.)* 🔑 OPAL A1
reaction *(n.)* 🔑 OPAL B1
reliable *(adj.)* 🔑 OPAL B1
sample *(n.)* 🔑 OPAL B1
trait *(n.)* B2

UNIT 2

account for *(v. phr.)* 🔑 OPAL B2
a function of *(n. phr.)* 🔑 OPAL
approximately *(adv.)* 🔑 OPAL B1
burn *(v.)* 🔑 A2
consume *(v.)* 🔑 OPAL B1
correlation *(n.)* OPAL C1

degree *(n.)* 🔑 OPAL A2
enjoy *(v.)* 🔑 A1
ethnic *(adj.)* OPAL B2
experiment *(v.)* 🔑 OPAL B1
feature *(n.)* 🔑 OPAL A2
illustrate *(v.)* 🔑 OPAL B2
key *(adj.)* 🔑 OPAL A1
local *(adj.)* 🔑 OPAL A1
play a role in *(v. phr.)* B2
rare *(adj.)* 🔑 B1
risk *(n.)* 🔑 OPAL B1
season *(v.)* 🔑 A2
spicy *(adj.)* 🔑 B1
with respect to *(prep. phr.)* OPAL C1

UNIT 3

as opposed to *(prep. phr.)* C1
cope *(v.)* B2
eventually *(adv.)* 🔑 B1
exhausted *(adj.)* B1
firsthand *(adv.)* C1
found *(v.)* 🔑 OPAL B2
influence *(n.)* 🔑 OPAL B1
informed *(adj.)* OPAL B2
permanent *(adj.)* 🔑 B2
put together *(v. phr.)* B2
quit *(v.)* 🔑 B1
research *(n.)* 🔑 OPAL A2
resource *(n.)* 🔑 OPAL B1

struggle *(v.)* 🔑 B2
support (oneself) *(v.)* 🔑
turn upside down *(v. phr.)* C1
unemployed *(adj.)* 🔑 B1
wages *(n.)* 🔑 B2

UNIT 4

add up to *(v. phr.)* B2
the bottom line *(n. phr.)* C1
character *(n.)* 🔑 OPAL A2
claim *(n.)* 🔑 OPAL B1
criticize *(v.)* 🔑 OPAL B2
disappear *(v.)* 🔑 A2
evidence *(n.)* 🔑 OPAL A2
give in *(v. phr.)* B1
infer *(v.)* OPAL B2
introduce *(v.)* 🔑 OPAL A1
merchandise *(n.)* C1
personal *(adj.)* 🔑 OPAL A1
regulate *(v.)* B2
scenario *(n.)* OPAL B2
take into account *(v. phr.)* B2
taste *(n.)* 🔑 A2
uncomfortable *(adj.)* 🔑 B1
unconsciously *(adv.)* B2
worldwide *(adj.)* 🔑 B1
willingness *(n.)* C1

UNIT 5

cycle *(n.)* OPAL A2
decline *(v.)* OPAL B2
development *(n.)* OPAL B1
discover *(v.)* OPAL A2
encourage *(v.)* OPAL B1
explore *(v.)* OPAL B1
financial *(adj.)* OPAL B1
growth *(n.)* OPAL B1
invention *(n.)* A2
investigate *(v.)* OPAL B1
judgment *(n.)* OPAL B2
locate *(v.)* OPAL B1
mystery *(n.)* B1
previous *(adj.)* OPAL B1
prove *(v.)* B1
reputation *(n.)* B2
retire *(v.)* B1
solve *(v.)* OPAL A2
survival *(n.)* OPAL B2
tendency *(n.)* OPAL B2

UNIT 6

automated *(adj.)* C1
be supposed to (do something)
  (v. phr.) B1
celebrity *(n.)* A2
clever *(adj.)* A2
companion *(n.)* C1

criterion *(n.)* OPAL B2
fair *(adj.)* A2
figure out *(v. phr.)* B2
genius *(n.)* B2
in this case *(adv. phr.)* B1
keep up with *(v. phr.)* B2
landscape *(n.)* B2
layer *(n.)* B1
obvious *(adj.)* OPAL B1
predictable *(adj.)* B2
program *(v.)* OPAL B1
reject *(v.)* OPAL B1
stand by *(v. phr.)* C2
take over *(v. phr.)* B2
take sides *(v. phr.)* C1

UNIT 7

acquire *(v.)* OPAL B2
analysis *(n.)* OPAL B1
associated with *(adj. phr.)* B2
burn out *(v. phr.)* C1
circumstances *(n.)* OPAL B2
complicated *(adj.)* B2
conduct *(v.)* OPAL B2
demonstrate *(v.)* OPAL B2
destructive *(adj.)* C1
dramatic *(adj.)* B2
get used to *(v. phr.)* B1
immediate *(adj.)* OPAL B1

independence *(n.)* OPAL B2
outcome *(n.)* OPAL B2
persuasive *(adj.)* B2
pleasure *(n.)* B1
somewhat *(adv.)* B2
wear off *(v. phr.)* C1
wholly *(adv.)* C1

UNIT 8

all along *(adv. phr.)* C1
award *(n.)* A2
blame *(v.)* B2
blind *(adj.)* B2
bring up *(v. phr.)* C1
convincing *(adj.)* B1
crash *(n.)* B2
disability *(n.)* B2
failure *(n.)* OPAL B2
give up *(v. phr.)* A2
go into *(v. phr.)* C1
highlight *(v.)* OPAL B1
incredibly *(adv.)* B1
innovate *(v.)* C1
inspiration *(n.)* C1
material *(n.)* OPAL A2
painful *(adj.)* B1
sincere *(adj.)* B2
supportive *(adj.)* C1
tricky *(adj.)* C1

AUTHORS AND CONSULTANTS

AUTHORS

Miles Craven has worked in English language education since 1988, teaching in private language schools, British Council centers, and universities in Italy, Portugal, Spain, Hong Kong, Japan, and the UK. He has a wide range of experience as a teacher, teacher trainer, examiner, course designer, and textbook writer. Miles is author or co-author of over 30 textbooks and regularly presents at conferences around the world. He also acts as Advisor for Executive Education programs at the Møller Centre for Continuing Education Ltd., Churchill College, University of Cambridge. His research focuses on helping students develop the skills and strategies they need to become confident communicators. He specializes in exam preparation for the TOEIC test.

Kristin Donnalley Sherman holds an M.Ed. in TESL from the University of North Carolina, Charlotte. She taught ESL/EFL at Central Piedmont Community College in Charlotte, North Carolina for twenty years, including grammar, reading, composition, listening, and speaking. She has written student books, teacher's editions, workbooks, and online content for adult and academic ESL/EFL. In addition, she has frequently presented at conferences and workshops internationally.

SERIES CONSULTANTS

Lawrence J. Zwier holds an M.A. in TESL from the University of Minnesota. He is currently the Associate Director for Curriculum Development at the English Language Center at Michigan State University in East Lansing. He has taught ESL/EFL in the United States, Saudi Arabia, Malaysia, Japan, and Singapore.

Marguerite Ann Snow holds a Ph.D. in Applied Linguistics from UCLA. She teaches in the TESOL M.A. program in the Charter College of Education at California State University, Los Angeles. She was a Fulbright scholar in Hong Kong and Cyprus. In 2006, she received the President's Distinguished Professor award at CSULA. She has trained ESL teachers in the United States and EFL teachers in more than 25 countries. She is the author/editor of numerous publications in the areas of content-based instruction, English for academic purposes, and standards for English teaching and learning. She is a co-editor of *Teaching English as a Second or Foreign Language* (4th ed.).

CRITICAL THINKING CONSULTANT **James Dunn** is a Junior Associate Professor at Tokai University and the Coordinator of the JALT Critical Thinking Special Interest Group. His research interests include Critical Thinking skills' impact on student brain function during English learning as measured by EEG. His educational goals are to help students understand that they are capable of more than they might think and to expand their cultural competence with critical thinking and higher-order thinking skills.

ASSESSMENT CONSULTANT **Elaine Boyd** has worked in assessment for over 30 years for international testing organizations. She has designed and delivered courses in assessment literacy and is also the author of several EL exam coursebooks for leading publishers. She is an Associate Tutor (M.A. TESOL/Linguistics) at University College, London. Her research interests are classroom assessment, issues in managing feedback, and intercultural competences.

VOCABULARY CONSULTANT **Cheryl Boyd Zimmerman** is Professor Emeritus at California State University, Fullerton. She specialized in second-language vocabulary acquisition, an area in which she is widely published. She taught graduate courses on second-language acquisition, culture, vocabulary, and the fundamentals of TESOL and has been a frequent invited speaker on topics related to vocabulary teaching and learning. She is the author of *Word Knowledge: A Vocabulary Teacher's Handbook* and Series Director of *Inside Reading, Inside Writing*, and *Inside Listening and Speaking* published by Oxford University Press.

ONLINE INTEGRATION **Chantal Hemmi** holds an Ed.D. TEFL and is a Japan-based teacher trainer and curriculum designer. Since leaving her position as Academic Director of the British Council in Tokyo, she has been teaching at the Center for Language Education and Research at Sophia University on an EAP/CLIL program offered for undergraduates. She delivers lectures and teacher trainings throughout Japan, Indonesia, and Malaysia.

COMMUNICATIVE GRAMMAR CONSULTANT **Nancy Schoenfeld** holds an M.A. in TESOL from Biola University in La Mirada, California, and has been an English language instructor since 2000. She has taught ESL in California and Hawaii, and EFL in Thailand and Kuwait. She has also trained teachers in the United States and Indonesia. Her interests include teaching vocabulary, extensive reading, and student motivation. She is currently an English Language Instructor at Kuwait University.